GOAL SETTING

SECOND EDITION

How to Create an Action Plan and Achieve Your Goals

Susan B. Wilson
and Michael S. Dobson

AMACOM

AMERICAN MANAGEMENT ASSOCIATION

New York • Atlanta • Brussels • Chicago • Mexico City • San Francisco
Shanghai • Tokyo • Toronto • Washington, D.C.

*This publication is designed to provide accurate and
authoritative information in regard to the subject matter
covered. It is sold with the understanding that the publisher is
not engaged in rendering legal, accounting, or other
professional service. If legal advice or other expert assistance
is required, the services of a competent professional person
should be sought.*

Library of Congress Cataloging-in-Publication Data

Wilson, Susan B.
    Goal setting : how to create an action plan and achieve your goals /
Susan B. Wilson and Michael S. Dobson. — 2nd ed.
        p.   cm. — (WorkSmart)
    Includes index.
    ISBN 978-0-8144-0169-9 (pbk.)
    1. Goal setting in personnel management.   2. Goal (Psychology)
3. Management—Psychological aspects.   4. Planning.   I. Dobson,
Michael Singer.   II. Title.

HF5549.5.G6W55   2008
650.1—dc22

                                                    2007039111

Printing number

10   9   8   7   6   5   4   3   2   1

CONTENTS

PREFACE TO THE SECOND EDITION

W hen people find out I've written several books, the first response is often, "Gee, I've always wanted to write a book." My first question is always the same, "Why?"

People are often puzzled at the question, but it's the most important question of all in setting and achieving your goals. You aren't chasing this goal for the fun of it, but because you believe achieving the goal will satisfy some need, solve some problem, or provide some benefit. If you can't clearly explain why you want to achieve the goal, there's a good chance you may head off in the wrong direction.

Let's apply the question to this particular goal: Why would someone want to write a book? Well, there are many possible reasons. Here are some of the more common ones:

(a) You want to make as much money as J. K. *(Harry Potter)* Rowling.
(b) You want to appear on *Oprah* and be famous.
(c) You want to impress people with your talent.
(d) You have something really important you want to share with the world.
(e) It's your art.
(f) It's your therapy.

For example, if your real goal is money, there are lots more reliable ways of getting it than by writing books. Yes, a few writers make an awful lot of money, but the vast majority of published authors make little or nothing. One writer I know devoted several years to writing a novel he *knew* would make a lot of money. He did well—achieving the Book of the Month Club, gaining foreign translations, and even selling the movie rights. But he wasn't satisfied. He expected to make millions. So he gave up. If you want to succeed at a goal, you need to understand why you want it. This is critical.

You have to do this process for any goal you set for yourself. Why do you want it? How does this goal relate to your other goals? What will be different for you when you succeed? Are there better ways to get there? What elements of the goal are the most valuable and the most important to you?

You'll learn in the pages of this book how to set a goal, how to make a plan, and how to acquire the resources and power necessary to achieve your goal. What you have to supply is the quality of your self-understanding. If you understand why, maybe you'll pursue the same goal, or maybe you'll change to a goal that actually relates more closely to what you hope to gain.

Knowing why gives you strength and power. If your goals are challenging (and they should be), achieving them takes hard work and risk. If the goal isn't really important to you or if you've picked a goal that won't really satisfy the "why," it's awfully difficult to maintain the self-discipline to get the job done.

A case in point: My best friend in college used to publish an amateur mimeographed magazine containing essays by a Pennsylvania schoolteacher who had sold a novel, quit his job, and let his wife support him. He was a good example of what *not* to do, or so I thought. For years, every time my friend and I got together and talked about old times, sooner or later one of us would ask, "What do you suppose ever *happened* to Dean Koontz?"

You probably already know how this story turns out. Dean Koontz has managed the rare feat of having ten *New York Times* number one bestsellers, and is still going strong. (His wife, I've read, still works: She manages their business.)

He knew what he wanted and why he wanted it, and so he was able to persist in the face of skepticism and rejection.

Always ask, "Why?" The more reasons you have to pursue a goal, the better you'll likely do in terms of achieving it. I write because I have a perspective on people and organizations that I want to share. But writing is not the only way to do that; I also teach seminars. I like the act of writing; I like seeing my books in bookstores.

Why do you want to achieve your goals? The answer to that question has power. It's what motivates you. It's what shows you the right path to take. And it's what opens the doors that lead to your success.

—Michael S. Dobson

PART I

1

SETTING PERSONAL GOALS

CHAPTER 1

GETTING STARTED

H ave you ever wondered why some people seem to have the ability to accomplish a lot? They know where they are headed and exude an enviable confidence. Effective goal setting is one of their keys to success. You may be working very hard at what you do, but without setting goals you'll find that your hard work doesn't yield meaningful results.

Remember *Alice in Wonderland*? At one point in the story, Alice stops at the crossroads to ask the Cheshire Cat which road to take. He responds by asking where she wants to go. When she tells him that she "doesn't much care where," he replies, "then it doesn't matter which way you go." As a result, she wanders aimlessly in her travels.

Like Alice, we often travel the road of life without a specific direction or goal. Few of us make goal setting a priority. In fact, studies have shown that most people either do not know what they want from life or, if they do, have no plans for realizing their dreams. Only a small percentage of people have specific, well-defined goals. And people who most frequently reach their goals are those who write them down and develop the plans to reach them.

Take a moment to consider why writing down your goals makes

such a significant difference in ultimate performance. Why do you think that writing down one's goals is so important?

If your response included the idea that goal achievers record their goals so that they can read them, absorb them, and plan for them, then you are on the right track. People who achieve their goals take an active role in achieving them. They write them down, and then plan for their achievement. This chapter considers ten guidelines for evaluating and writing down your goals. If you follow these guidelines, you will establish your goals in a way that nearly guarantees your effort will be rewarded. Time and again, your reward is successful goal achievement.

Before learning the ten guidelines for effective goal setting, take a few minutes to identify two of your goals—they can be anything as long as they are meaningful to you—and write them down. Then, complete the self-audit, which identifies ten elements for effective goal setting. Evaluate the extent to which you use these ideas when developing your goals.

Your Goals

1. _____

2. _____

Now complete the self-audit on page 5 by checking either "Nearly Always," "Sometimes," or "Rarely" for each statement.

TEN GUIDELINES THAT REALLY WORK

The questions you just answered identify ten guidelines for effective goal setting. Using these ideas ensures that you establish goals that can be accomplished. The ten guidelines are:

1. **Effective goals are written.** Many of us daydream about what we would like to accomplish. But how many of us pick up a pen and write down those things we most want to achieve? Once a dream is committed to paper, it becomes concrete. Your dream is

given a sense of reality. **Writing down your goals is a first step toward achieving them.**

SELF-AUDIT FOR GOAL SETTING

	Nearly Always	Sometimes	Rarely
1. When I set a goal, I write it down.			
2. I describe my goal in specific, measurable terms.			
3. I often visualize my goals.			
4. My goals are achievable.			
5. I set realistic deadlines for completing my goals.			
6. I break a large goal into manageable units.			
7. I look for the potential problems that may keep me from reaching my goals.			
8. I take action to remove or minimize those potential problems.			
9. I review progress toward my goals on a regular basis.			
10. I know the personal rewards of reaching my goals.			

Assess your responses by counting the number of times you responded "Nearly Always" and multiply that number by 3. Multiply the number of times you responded "Sometimes" by 2, and the number of times you responded "Rarely" by 1. Then add the resulting three numbers for a total score.

Nearly Always   _____ (number of responses) × 3 = _____
Sometimes   _____ (number of responses) × 2 = _____
Rarely   _____ (number of responses) × 1 = _____
GRAND TOTAL = _____

Analyzing Your Score

Score of:

24–30   Excellent job of setting effective goals. If you find that you do an excellent job of setting goals, but you feel you could be more successful in reaching them, then Chapter 2 may be especially meaningful for you.

18–23 You are on your way to achieving effective goal setting. Take another look at the statements where your responses were less than "Nearly Always." These are the areas for additional concentration.

Below 18 There are several areas in which you can improve your goal setting. In setting the goal of reading and using this book, you are becoming a more effective goal setter.

2. **Effective goals are written in specific, measurable terms.** If you write your goal in specific terms, then you probably have expressed it in a measurable way. A goal needs to be measurable so that your progress can be evaluated and so that you will know when you have achieved your goal. For instance, you may think about learning a new computer software package. But only when you describe your goal as "taking a class in WordPerfect between March and June and spending six to eight hours a week to learn its applications to my job" will you have a definable, measurable goal.

EXAMPLES OF MEASURABLE GOALS

■ By April 1, I will have my taxes completed and ready to be mailed.

■ This week I will make fifteen sales calls and close on four of them.

■ We will hire a new secretary within two weeks.

3. **Effective goals can be visualized.** Picture yourself reaching your goal. Picture the result, the moment, and your feelings. Much of our energy for reaching goals comes from a desire to attain them. Usually, the more you desire something, the harder you will work toward achieving it. For example, a sales rep has won several awards. He accomplishes his extraordinary sales goals by visualizing his reward of receiving the plaque and winning the trip each year. He says, "I can see myself walking across the stage, being congratulated by the CEO, and enjoying my moment in the spotlight. When I'm having a slow day, I just visualize the result that I want, and it renews my energy."

Victor Frankl is a Viennese psychologist and survivor of a World War II concentration camp. In his book *Man's Search for Mean-*

ing, Frankl describes people who were able to visualize their goals for living and, consequently, were able to withstand the tortures of their circumstances. He maintains that people who had no purpose died quickly; those who kept an eye on their goals were more likely to survive.

. . . .

4. **Effective goals are achievable.** Goals need to challenge your skills and abilities, without discouraging your effort and performance. For example, when initially implementing a quality management program, companies do not usually target the highly acclaimed and highly competitive Malcolm Baldrige National Quality Award as their first goal. Instead, they establish less stringent quality goals at first so that work teams can experience success in reaching those more realistic goals. As competency, success, and confidence grow, work teams may then decide to stretch for the higher goal.

5. **Effective goals have realistic deadlines.** Goals need a schedule. You are more likely to take action when you set a realistic time frame for accomplishing your goal. Schedule enough time to reach the goal, but not so much time that you lose interest in it. How many people have you heard say they need a vacation from their work but don't get around to taking one? A far higher percentage of people meet their goal when they record their specific intentions. "I will plan a vacation for the second week in March and arrangements will be settled by January 15."

6. **Effective goals are manageable.** Sometimes a goal can seem overwhelming because of its size. But if it is divided into smaller components, then it becomes easier to manage and is achievable. To hear your boss say that he wants you to open seventy-two accounts this year may sound unrealistic, but if you think of it in terms of six accounts each month, then the goal is more manageable.

7. **Effective goals are analyzed for their potential problems.** As you establish a goal, consider the steps you must take to accomplish it. Analyze the goal for potential problems that might keep you from reaching it. If a goal initially is considered in terms of what could go wrong, then you can take action to resolve or minimize problems before they occur. Critical thinking helps you cover all the angles and stay on the path toward achieving your goal.

. . . .

ANALYZE YOUR GOAL FOR POTENTIAL PROBLEMS

What could go wrong with the goal of "Meeting a Project Dead-line"?

1. A member on the project team does not complete his or her part on time.
2. A needed piece of equipment may break down (e.g., word processor).
3. Unexpected tasks related to the project may arise.
4. The supervisor may not like the format of the final result.

. . . .

8. **Effective goals require action to eliminate or minimize the consequences of potential problems.** This is the follow-through for identifying potential problems. At this point, you iden-tify the *action* that is required to either remove the cause of the problem or minimize its consequences. For example, an unproduc-tive team member could be the cause of a potential problem. Elimi-nate the problem by removing the unproductive member from the team. Other potential problems, however, can be dealt with only by minimizing their impact. For example, in manufacturing there is often a potential for equipment breakdown. Minimize the conse-quences by providing regular maintenance or having backup equip-ment available.

9. **Effective goals include a regular review of progress.** A periodic review of your goals will help ensure that they continue to be realistic, timely, and relevant. Consider, for example, the human resources director who, only twelve credit hours and a dissertation away from her doctorate, decided to quit. How could she invest the time, money, and energy to get so far toward a goal and then quit? After serious review of her career, family, and financial goals, she realized that the degree did not hold the promise it once had. Ob-taining a doctorate was no longer a relevant goal for her life circum-stances and interests.

10. **Effective goals yield rewards that are of value to you.** We stay motivated to work toward our goals when we know and desire the resulting rewards, whatever they may be. As you establish each goal, identify at least one meaningful reward for yourself. It may be money, recognition, a day off, or the quiet pleasure you feel

for a job done well. Your reward can be anything of value to you, something that motivates your effort to accomplish the goal. Without recognizing specific benefits that accrue as a result of your efforts, the probability of reaching that goal decreases.

With these ten points in mind, review the two goals you wrote on page 4. Consider the extent to which you can use the ten guidelines just discussed.

Which of the guidelines are the most difficult for you to use?

_____

_____

_____

_____

Keeping the guidelines in mind, how would you rewrite your goals?

_____

_____

_____

_____

Goals provide direction for your life; they focus your activities. Goals are the points on your roadmap where you can apply your talents and energies. Without well-constructed goals, your life is governed by whim or the urgency of the moment. But effective goals will provide you with the internal control to make things happen the way you want them to.

DO YOUR GOALS SHOW YOU THE WAY?

At the beginning of this chapter, you listed two goals to jump-start your thinking. Then you were given ten guidelines to help you consider those goals in a more systematic way. For the next exercise, review the areas of life listed next for which effective goal setting is critical. Check those areas for which you already have significant goals. Then write down those goals using the worksheet. If you need to, refer to the goal-setting guidelines to help you stay on track.

Life Areas

Place a check mark by those areas in which you want to write goals.

❑   **Spiritual**

❑   **Personal development**

❑   **Leisure time**

❑   **Professional**

❑   **Civic/community**

❑   **Family**

❑   **Social**

❑   **Health/physical well-being**

❑   **Educational**

❑   **Financial**

❑   **Other** _____

_____

_____

GOALS WORKSHEET

Life Area _____
Goals

1. _____

2. _____

3. _____

Life Area _____
Goals

1. _____

2. _____

3. _____

Life Area _____
Goals

1. _____

2. _____

3. _____

Life Area _____
Goals

1. _____

2. _____

3. _____

Life Area _____
Goals

1. _____

2. _____

3. _____

Life Area _____
Goals

1. _____

2. _____

3. _____

CHAPTER 2

POTENTIAL OBSTACLES TO REACHING YOUR GOALS

S uppose you know what you want, and you are on the right track to accomplishing your goals. Without warning, you suddenly face an obstacle that blocks your progress. And then it is difficult to remain focused and energetic. If you do nothing about the obstacles that arise, they can sap your energy, your time, and your enthusiasm. Consider the following list of obstacles that could block you from accomplishing your goals.

- I need to feel secure.
- I may fail.
- I doubt my skills.
- Changing the way I do things is not easy.
- I have too many things to do.

Each of these is a potential barrier you set up yourself to defeat your effort. But there are strategies for removing them—or at least for minimizing their impact.

I NEED TO FEEL SECURE

Many of us fear that if we try something new, we may lose our sense of security. We enjoy the security of life as we know it. The irony is that this security can change at a moment's notice.

A major layoff at work, a storm that destroys your community, a personal tragedy—these events can put your security at risk and quickly alter your life. You don't have the power to control all the elements that can potentially affect you. So, a more dependable course of action is to build an internal security system within yourself. Instead of trying to grasp at an intangible security that could change momentarily, develop the coping skills that are so essential for life in a world of probable changes. Effective coping skills usually include the ability to handle stressful events, the ability to take calculated risks, and the ability to manage problems as they arise. An internal security system, built through effective coping skills, will help you make reasoned choices. You will find that the fear of giving up security will diminish as an obstacle to your success.

. . . .

A middle manager who enjoyed the security of a hefty paycheck and company benefits also faced the strain of a dead-end job. His daily work lacked challenge, and it was not likely he would receive another promotion. He decided to weigh the merits of continuing in a secure but lackluster job versus the risk of seeking new challenges. After a six-month job search, he found a position that was a better fit with his talents and interests. And in the process, he developed the internal strengths of initiative, confidence, and improved interviewing skills. Just three months into his new position, he learned that several middle management positions, including his former position, had been eliminated at his former employer. For him, this was a lesson in how quickly one's perceived security can change, and how important it is to develop the personal strength to cope with life's changing circumstances and inherent risks.

. . . .

Are you willing to give up some of your perceived security to accomplish a goal? If not, why not?

_____

_____

Do you agree that to "not change a thing" can be a risk? Why?

_____

_____

Which of your goals seems risky? Why?

_____

_____

Thinking About Risk

There are several ways to increase your level of comfort and manage the perceived risk associated with meeting one of your goals:

■ Specify the risk you associate with the particular goal under consideration. Identify how large that risk really is. If its potential impact is low, then rational thought suggests that the risk is minimal.

■ Determine the probability of that risk occurring. Is it very likely, somewhat likely, or not very likely at all? Unless the probability of occurrence is fairly high, your energy and time are better spent addressing higher-risk issues.

■ Identify the benefits that accrue from taking the risk and succeeding. After you determine the probability and degree of the risk, you may decide that the anticipated benefits outweigh the potential disadvantages.

■ Once you identify the probability and impact of the risk, and the benefits from pursuing the goal, there may be added advantage in seeking input from a friend or adviser.

. . . .

Several years ago, the new president of a company that manufactures plastics established a goal that had a low probability of serious risk but large potential financial benefits. The company wanted to sell polyurethane products to the oil and gas industry. Unfortunately, following the company's investment of $500,000 into the proposed product, the oil industry collapsed unexpectedly, and the investment was lost. Although it was a calculated risk, the company's president maintains that he used the failure as a learning opportunity. Instead of bemoaning his loss, he turned to his internal security system. He used well-honed problem-solving and stress-management skills to learn from the situation. As a result, he found other opportunities to pursue, and he maintained his ability to take other risks that have led to profitable products.

. . . .

I MAY FAIL

When is the last time you failed at something? Was it truly a failure or were you able to learn from the situation? No one enjoys the feeling of failure, but often we are overly critical and extra-hard on ourselves. And once we feel that we have failed, we replay the incident in our mind until we view ourselves as failures instead of having one failed goal. If you fail to reach a goal, view the situation objectively. Avoid harboring negative emotions and feelings. Instead, identify what went well and what could have been done better. Identify opportunities to apply what you learned.

In trying to avoid failure, you may miss the adventure of personal growth, the fun of meeting a new challenge, or the excitement of living for those things in which you believe. Abraham Lincoln and Thomas Edison are examples of men who took risks and "failed" many times to reach their goals.

They used their failures as learning experiences and were not deterred from continuing to set goals. Instead, each man held to a belief in himself as he continued to pursue the goals in which he so strongly believed.

Think for a moment about an experience that you consider a failure and write it down.

_____

_____

What feelings did you have about it?

_____

_____

Did the experience offer opportunities for personal growth? What were they?

_____

_____

Do you agree that you are better prepared for coping with the challenges of life for having had that experience?

_____

_____

Thinking About the Fear of Failure

Here are some ideas to help you reduce your fear of failure:

■ Confront your fear of failure. Why do you feel this way? Is this particular fear justified? If it is, what can you do to eliminate or reduce your fear?

■ Look at your failure from a new perspective. Failing to reach a goal does not make *you* a failure. It only means that you did not reach that goal.

. . . .

A promising junior executive at a blue-chip corporation lost several million dollars of that company's money in a new venture. The company's president and founder summoned the executive to his office. Trembling, he stood in front of the president and said, "I guess you want my resignation." Without hesitation, the president replied, "You can't be serious. We've just spent millions of dollars educating you." This rising star was being reminded of the opportunity to learn from failure and to use the experience as a springboard for renewed effort toward company goals.

. . . .

■ Know that there are benefits of having taken specific steps involved in working toward a goal even if you fail to reach the goal. One benefit is the practical education of making the effort. Another is the opportunity to practice specific skills. A third is the recognition that meeting some goals and failing to meet others is part of the ebb and flow of life.

■ Recognize that you probably will not achieve significant goals without some failures. Failing provides unique learning opportunities that ultimately contribute to your personal growth and to your organizational contribution.

I DOUBT MY SKILLS

Do you have a strong commitment to reaching your goals? If not, this lack of commitment may weaken your confidence in your own skills and abilities. You think to yourself, "I think I can do this, but

I'm really not sure." Since the manner in which you mentally talk to yourself impacts your performance, it is important to focus on your strengths. Identify your abilities in a positive way. Focus on the things that you do well. Then decide which skills need work and identify strategies for improving these. Taking positive specific action will help you develop confidence in your skills and abilities.

. . . .

An insurance company decided to apply for the Malcolm Baldrige National Quality Award. In that year, sixty-six companies competed. The company was judged as one of the two best service organizations in the United States, but it did not meet the goal of winning the national award. Far from viewing their effort as a failure, employees celebrated their commitment to quality, appreciated what they had learned in the award process, and were grateful for the feedback regarding their quality improvement program.

. . . .

Do you lack confidence in your skills or abilities to reach a goal? If yes, why?

_____

_____

What will you do to increase your confidence?

_____

_____

How will you renew a commitment to your goal?

_____

_____

Thinking About Increasing Your Confidence

Here are some ideas to help you build confidence in your skills and abilities:

■ Think specifically and positively about your skills and abilities. Identify how they can contribute to each of your goals. Write these down.

■ Keeping your skills and abilities in mind, establish a realistic standard of achievement for your goal.

■ Establish a step-by-step plan for reaching your goal so that you can mark your progress.

■ When trying something new, think in terms of specific skills or behaviors that need changing. Avoid generalizations. Instead of "I'm terrible at running a meeting," try "I need to develop and use an agenda."

■ Avoid the exclusive use of others' opinions when evaluating your skills. Include your beliefs and your opinions as you make decisions about changes that need to be made.

■ For each criticism that you give yourself, also give yourself one or two specific compliments.

CHANGING THE WAY I DO THINGS IS NOT EASY

Do you enjoy change? If so, you probably are in the minority. Change is uncomfortable for most of us, even when it is for the better. Change means letting go of what is familiar. When we do that, we face the challenge of coping with new ideas and situations. But as much as you may resist change, it cannot be stopped. Your challenge is to accept that change is inevitable, so that your resources are used in concert with that change. Working against change often can be stressful, while working with and through change is a source of energy and greater strength. When you strive toward new goals, often you must change in some way. If you view change as a catalyst for reaching those goals, you will be better able to accept change with a more grateful perspective.

Which of your most significant goals require you to change in some way?

_____

_____

In what ways do you need or want to change?

_____

_____

Thinking About Managing Change

Here are some ideas to help you face change:

■ If change is a problem, admit it. Often, a first step to dealing with a problem is to admit that it exists.

■ If possible, experience change gradually. Handling change all at once is tougher than easing into it. Many people find that they can even schedule the changes that they must accept.

■ Try seeking change as opposed to its seeking you. This will give you a sense of greater control over your future.

■ See yourself as someone who looks forward to change. Try new foods or new activities and seek new acquaintances. Doing so establishes a pattern of willingness to experience the new.

I HAVE TOO MANY THINGS TO DO

Frequently, there _are_ too many things to do. Fortunately, you have the ability to prioritize your goals and activities. Review your list of goals at the end of Chapter 1. Which are the most important to you? Which give you the greatest return on your investment? Which provide you with the greatest enjoyment or sense of accomplishment? Use your responses to prioritize the goals that are the most important to you. Then plan your hours, your days, and even your months to reach those goals.

In working on tasks, ignore the trivial and concentrate on the vital.

Thinking About Prioritizing Your Goals

The following steps will help you put your goals in order of priority:

1. Identify criteria for prioritizing your goals. For example, which are the most important to you? Which have the greatest impact?

2. Use a high-medium-low scale to assess your goals, using your criteria.

3. Make those goals with the highest rankings your high-priority items.

Most of us realize that effective goal setting is a key to getting things accomplished. However, as we have reviewed in this chapter, there are potential obstacles that impede progress. Only when you understand the nature of the obstacles confronting you can you develop strategies to minimize these and achieve your goals.

CHAPTER 3

ELEVEN STRATEGIES TO OPTIMIZE REACHING YOUR GOALS

A lthough reaching your goals cannot be guaranteed, raise the probability of achieving them with the eleven strategies discussed in this chapter.

Before reading on, review the questions on the next page and mark your responses. Then score yourself using the information that follows the questions.

KNOW THE RESOURCES REQUIRED FOR REACHING A GOAL

Personal desire for reaching a goal is powerful, but often other resources are needed as well. What resources do you need to reach your goals—time, money, position? Additional education? The help of a particular person?

For example, consider the goal of purchasing a computer system for your home office. The resources you might need include: money to purchase the computer, the software, and the printer; additional knowledge for knowing how to use it; and the help of a computer consultant.

Now, consider one of your goals. What specific resources are needed for its achievement?

Goal: _____

Resources Required: _____

ELEVEN STRATEGIES FOR GOAL SETTING

	Often	Sometimes	Rarely/ Never
1. I know what resources I need to reach my goals.	_____	_____	_____
2. I work toward goals that are compatible with one another.	_____	_____	_____
3. I am comfortable asking for help to reach my goals.	_____	_____	_____
4. I accept the responsibility for working toward my goals.	_____	_____	_____
5. I minimize interruptions that get in the way of reaching my goals.	_____	_____	_____
6. I am flexible to changes that affect my progress toward my goals.	_____	_____	_____
7. I know the benefits of reaching my goals.	_____	_____	_____
8. I am persistent about working toward my goals.	_____	_____	_____
9. I review my progress toward my goals on a regular basis.	_____	_____	_____
10. I achieve a balance of effort between the goals that are important to me.	_____	_____	_____
11. I only pursue those activities that are related to reaching my goals.	_____	_____	_____

Assess your responses to this exercise by counting the number of times that you responded "Often" and multiply that number by 3. Multiply the number of times that you responded "Sometimes" by 2, and the number of times that you responded "Rarely/Never" by 1. Then add the resulting three numbers for a total score.

Often   _____ (number of responses) $\times$ 3 = _____
Sometimes   _____ (number of responses) $\times$ 2 = _____
Rarely/Never   _____ (number of responses) $\times$ 1 = _____
                                                       Grand Total = _____

Analyzing Your Score

Score of:

33–39   You have a healthy understanding of what it takes to see your goals accomplished.

26–32   You are well on your way to developing the personal discipline for reaching your goals.

19–25   You will find the information in this chapter useful as you sharpen the skills for reaching your goals.

Strategies for Staying Power

The statements to which you responded relate to strategies that encourage your "staying power" when working toward a goal. Most of us benefit from strategies that strengthen our resolve. Each of these strategies is discussed in detail in this chapter. As you read, note your areas of strength as well as opportunities for improvement.

WORK WITH GOALS THAT ARE COMPATIBLE

When goals conflict with one another they compete for your time, energy, and personal resources, which can leave you feeling drained and stressed. For example, a manager was challenged by his boss to spend more time on the production floor interacting with his employees, and then was criticized for not spending enough time at his desk. To him, these two goals were in conflict with one another.

Another example is the manager who wanted to complete her doctorate. She enrolled at a university and was beginning her studies when she learned that she was pregnant. In analyzing the situation, she discovered that the goals of pursuing an education, maintaining a full-time job, and starting a family were not compatible at that time. Trying to meet the challenges of these goals would deplete her resources of energy, time, and enthusiasm.

Review your goals. Which ones are competing for your resources? How can you modify or change your goals so that they are more compatible?

_____

_____

BE WILLING TO ASK FOR HELP WITH YOUR GOALS

Many people are willing to help you if you ask for their assistance. Specify your needs and identify specific ways in which others can help. Remember, part of the way you can repay the help you receive is to be a resource for others.

Whose skills, knowledge, and/or gifts can help you reach one or more of your goals?

_____

_____

Which of your skills, knowledge, and/or gifts can you use to help someone else?

_____

_____

ACCEPT THE RESPONSIBILITY FOR DOING THE WORK THAT IS NECESSARY TO REACH YOUR GOALS

Establishing goals is a start. Accepting the responsibility to accomplish them is another challenge. When the going gets tough, many people begin to blame others for their lack of progress. Instead of getting caught in a defensive, blaming trap, apply your time and energy to solving problems, making decisions, and working your plan so that your goals are realized.

How do you typically react when faced with a problem?

_____

_____

Does your reaction get in the way of your potential success?

_____

_____

Are you willing to change your behavior? If so, how?

_____

_____

MINIMIZE THE INTERRUPTIONS THAT BLOCK YOUR PROGRESS TOWARD YOUR GOALS

Many interruptions have the appearance of urgency and importance, but often they are time wasters and trivial matters. When an interruption arises, quickly evaluate it in terms of its importance to your goals. If it is not an enabler to your progress, then it may be a hindrance.

Do you control interruptions or do interruptions control you?

_____

_____

Do you handle interruptions swiftly and decisively?

_____

_____

What specific actions can you take to minimize the interruptions to your day?

_____

_____

BE FLEXIBLE TO CHANGES THAT AFFECT YOUR PROGRESS TOWARD A GOAL

Although a planned path optimizes progress toward your goals, the unexpected does sometimes arise and can either impede or facilitate progress. When an unforeseen change in your plan occurs, evaluate it for damage control. Brainstorm alternatives to eliminate or minimize the impact of the problem, but also look for opportunities!

· ·

An advertising agency that was growing quickly felt several pressures affecting its progress toward its five-year goal of becoming known nationally for creative thinking. The company's president died unexpectedly, a multimillion-dollar account was lost, the economy forced several other clients to drop the services, and several key management people left the company. Instead of allowing these changes to debilitate the company, agency executives sought opportunities in the challenges. They streamlined the agency, recommitted themselves to a vision of what the agency could be, and sought outside assistance to strengthen skills.

· ·

What are the potential problems or changes that could get in the way of reaching one of your goals?

_____

_____

What actions will you take to optimize your opportunities and minimize potential problems?

Action to Optimize   Action to Minimize

_____   _____

_____   _____

IDENTIFY THE BENEFITS OF REACHING YOUR GOALS

Get tuned into WII-FM (What's in It for Me?). Knowing and wanting the goal's benefits is a key factor in motivating you to apply your time, energy, and resources. No salesperson is successful without an effort to sell the benefits of a product or a service to the client. So sell your goal's benefits to yourself. Perhaps the benefits include exposure to upper management, a chance to learn something new, or the opportunity for a promotion. When you value the benefit that you'll receive, that value increases your motivation to reach the goal.

What factors motivate you to work toward a particular goal?

_____

_____

What are the benefits of reaching one or more of your goals?

_____

_____

DEVELOP THE PERSISTENCE TO WORK TOWARD YOUR GOALS

Persistence may be the most important quality for reaching your goals. Many people are willing to quit when the going gets rough. What about you? Are you willing to make short-term sacrifices in order to accomplish something that is meaningful to you?

Consider your goals. On a scale of 1 to 10 (10 = high), how important are your goals to you?

_____

_____

If you believe that they are important, do you have the persistence to work toward your goals?

_____

_____

REVIEW YOUR PROGRESS TOWARD YOUR GOALS REGULARLY

Reviewing your goals not only identifies the progress you've made, but also provides an opportunity to ensure that you are on track and that you have adequate resources at your disposal. A review of your goals also fans the fire of motivation by highlighting your accomplishments. Consider posting a list of your goals so you can see them on a daily basis. Charting your progress regularly is also motivating.

Do you make a point of reviewing your goals on a regular basis?

_____

_____

Would charting your progress increase your motivation?

_____

_____

BALANCE YOUR EFFORTS AMONG THE GOALS THAT ARE IMPORTANT TO YOU

Often we find ourselves applying a disproportionate amount of time to certain goals. One successful realtor who sold 7 million dollars' worth of real estate in a year realized that while she said that her family was very important to her, in reality she did not share much of her time and energy with them. Instead, most of her resources went to her job. Those long hours might ensure job performance, but goals related to other areas of life (family, friends, community, or spiritual life) may suffer.

In Chapter 1 you identified goals related to different areas of your life. Do you apply adequate amounts of time, energy, and resources to each of those areas that are important to you? If not, what changes are you willing to make?

_____

_____

REACH YOUR GOALS BY CONCENTRATING ON THOSE THINGS THAT RELATE TO YOUR GOALS

Whatever activities are planned in your day, consider their value to reaching your goals. Frequently, there are activities that you can eliminate or modify so that you can concentrate on making progress toward your significant goals.

Are you willing to give priority to those activities that contribute specifically to your goals? How can you do this?

_____

_____

Experiencing progress toward goals that are meaningful to you is gratifying and can motivate you toward even more accomplishments. Using these eleven strategies nearly guarantees progress toward reaching your goals. Prepare to reap the benefits of your effort!

2

EFFECTIVE GOAL SETTING AND PEOPLE SKILLS

CHAPTER 4

ASSERTIVE BEHAVIOR

H ow often have you felt frustrated by a difficulty to express yourself clearly and concisely? Have you tried to express your goals to a colleague and then realized that your colleague didn't understand you? Do you wish that you could communicate more effectively? By being assertive, you convey your needs and goals in a clear and direct manner. Assertiveness is a communication style that confirms your right to be heard, but in a caring and respectful manner toward others. The more clearly and reasonably you express your goals, the more likely others will understand them. And as others understand your needs, they are more likely to help you attain your goals.

Assertiveness often is misunderstood. Frequently the word conjures up an image of a meek person suddenly changed into a tough individual. A popular cartoon shows a man looking tentatively at a door labeled, "Assertiveness Training, Barge Right In." Although funny, the cartoon illustrates the dilemma concerning assertiveness: People often associate assertive behavior with aggressive behavior.

Assertive behavior is an honest expression of your opinions, feelings, and beliefs. It is behavior that demonstrates your right to be treated with dignity and respect. Assertiveness is evidenced through your words, behavior, and actions. For example, imagine that you are one of ten participants at a meeting scheduled for 3:00 P.M. At 3:10 P.M., two of the participants have not yet arrived. Although you are not the chairperson, you want the meeting to start so as to: (1) minimize the cost of wasted time, (2) have the opportunity to contribute to the meeting, and (3) leave by 4:00 P.M. so that you can get to your 4:10 appointment on time. Instead of staying quiet and inwardly fuming, you say to the chairperson, "It's 3:10. Since most of us are here let's get started so that we can finish on time." Your statement raises the probability of achieving your goals while at the same time respects the time of others.

Honesty regarding your thoughts, opinions, and feelings is integral to assertive behavior, but so is showing respect and concern for others. The key difference between assertiveness and aggressiveness is that the assertive person accepts others' needs and goals while the aggressive person does not.

There are no absolute guidelines for cultivating assertive behavior. However, there are a number of ways you can work on this skill:

1. **Practice, practice, practice.** Communication is dynamic. New situations, new people, varied moods, and deeper insights challenge your ability to communicate honestly, clearly, and respectfully. Begin to flex your assertive behavior in nonthreatening, low-risk situations. Consider, for example, your need to confront two situations at work. The first involves a coworker who consistently leaves your computer on after she borrows it. The other is your boss, who either yells or gives you the cold shoulder when a mistake occurs. Which situation would *you* choose to deal with first? Probably the forgetful coworker, in order to build a reservoir of successfully using assertive behavior. As you feel more confident with your assertiveness, you will be more effective when confronting riskier situations, such as an overbearing boss.

2. **Consider the situation.** Be aware of what is going on around you. For example, consider the salesperson who travels internationally to service his accounts. In the United States, it is assertive for him to be direct in his sales presentation. And it is assertive to ask for the sale at the close of the presentation. However, in Japan, this situation probably would be perceived very differently—directness is viewed as pushy and aggressive. Japanese culture requires an emphasis on relationship and process. What is

accepted as assertive behavior in the United States very likely is perceived as aggressive in Japan.

3. **Avoid hurting others.** "What a stupid idea" may be an honest expression of thought, but it has the potential of hurting the feelings of the other party. When you are in doubt about how your communication might be understood, ask yourself: "Would I feel comfortable if someone were talking to me in this way?" and "Is my communication honest and direct, but given in a caring manner?"

In a meeting, someone establishes a goal that you think is without merit. How do you express your view in an honest, but fair and respectful way?

---

4. **Treat everyone with respect and dignity.** An assertive person treats those involved in the communication process with respect and dignity because they are deserving of those rights as people, not because of an organizational hierarchy, a false sense of status, or a difference in credentials, background, or experiences. An assertive individual, whether speaking with a housekeeper or the president of a company, makes it a practice to treat people with courtesy and respect. Your attention to the dignity of all people empowers you to reach your goals. When you are recognized as someone who respects people, others are more willing to help you reach your goals because they believe that you will care about their goals as well.

Your assertive behavior encourages assertive behavior in others. If you behave in an open, honest, and direct manner, and treat others with dignity and respect, then people are likely to respond in the same way. Even when a confrontation is initially aggressive, your assertive response can guide the communication toward mutual honesty and respect. If the aggression continues in spite of your best efforts, however, an assertive response might be, "I can see that you are quite angry. We can reschedule this discussion when we both feel calmer." In doing so, you don't allow the other party to treat you in a less than respectful manner.

People who use their assertiveness skills report feeling an increased sense of personal power. They feel more confident, more likable, and more respected. Another outcome is that they are more likely to achieve their goals as well as contribute to the goals of others.

YOU HAVE A CHOICE

We operate on a behavioral continuum that is dynamic and that includes three kinds of behaviors: assertive, aggressive, and passive. Our movement along the continuum is affected by the situations in which we find ourselves. The environment, the mood, and the people involved affect the choices we make regarding our behavior. Optimally, assertive behavior is most frequently chosen. Neither the passive nor the aggressive style optimizes the achievement of goals. Passive behavior tends to defer to others. A person choosing this style treats others with respect, but doesn't expect others to return that respect—and therefore often they don't. Aggressive behavior, on the other hand, demands attention from others. People with an aggressive style expect respect from others and make their goals known, but they are insensitive to the goals and needs of others.

Consistent use of either the passive or the aggressive style increases the risk of alienating people and losing their support, which is critical to accomplishing goals. Developing assertive behavior is a habit that can be cultivated if you choose to do so. Let's look more closely at these three behavioral styles.

Passive Behavior

For many, passive behavior is a way to avoid conflict. The passive behavioral style suppresses personal needs in order to get along with others. It also avoids taking personal responsibility to establish and communicate goals. Passive behavior often includes rambling thoughts, apologetic words, indirect speech, and silence. People with a passive style hope that others can guess their needs. Goals, if reached, are accomplished in a random fashion because they are not expressed clearly and assertively.

Over time, however, other people become frustrated trying to communicate with a passive person. The often unclear and ambiguous communication means that the listener interprets the information to meet his or her own needs. As a result, the passive person is easily hurt, disappointed, and even angry about interactions, and tends to avoid situations that seem risky or confrontational.

Describe a time when you chose to use a passive style of behavior.

_____

_____

How did you feel?

_____

_____

Did you accomplish your goal?

_____

_____

Aggressive Behavior

The person with an aggressive style expresses thoughts and feelings loudly and clearly, but often does not welcome that same honest expression from others. The person with aggressive behavior often demonstrates a loss of self-control as he or she demands control of a situation in order to meet goals. Anger, sarcasm, arrogance, and even outbursts are used. Situations are either win or lose, and the aggressive individual intends to emerge as the winner. An aggressive person is recognized by a tense demanding voice, narrowed staring eyes, rigid posture, and abrupt gestures. He or she may intimidate and accomplish goals in the short run; however, the anger and hostility that this behavior creates in others diminish the opportunities for accomplishing long-term goals.

Describe a time when you used aggressive behavior.

_____

_____

How did you feel?

_____

_____

How would you choose to handle a similar situation in an assertive way?

_____

_____

Assertive Behavior

Sending a message of acceptance, assertive behavior is expressive of personal wants and needs, but seeks that same expression from others, with a willingness to listen and understand. In this way, the assertive person is emotionally honest about equalizing the power in a relationship. The assertive person speaks in a personalized, direct manner. He or she tends to be persuasive because the interactions are honest, supportive, and clear.

Personal characteristics of assertiveness include a friendly, relaxed voice; eye contact; relaxed posture; and relaxed, open gestures. This style is self-perpetuating in that it demonstrates warmth and respect for others and encourages the same. The assertive person embraces confidence, self-respect, and personal caring as well as caring for others. The ability to recognize and work for positive outcomes is an asset of the assertive person. Consequently, this is a person who frequently accomplishes personal goals.

If you decide to use an assertive style of communication more frequently, what will be the positive outcomes for you?

_____

_____

Frequently, your interactions with others are goal-related. You need to know how to communicate effectively with others so that they will start or keep doing those things that are helpful to you. Assertiveness provides a method for doing so by using communication that is honest, direct, and respectful.

Developing Assertive Messages

There are three components to delivering an effective assertive message:

1. Identify the real issue, and develop a specific description of the behavior.

2. Express your feelings about that behavior to the person who can take action.

3. Describe the positive or the negative consequences of that behavior.

For example, imagine that one of your colleagues is continually late for meetings. By describing the behavior, the concern is more easily understood by your listener. For example, it is more specific to say, "You have been fifteen minutes late three times this week" than to say, "You are always late." While you can time someone's appearance on the job, it is difficult to document that someone is "always late." Rarely are absolute words true. Words such as *always, never, totally, absolutely, every,* and *constantly* are best left unused unless you can document their accuracy.

. . . .

ASSERTIVE RESPONSES

Read the following situations and identify each as an example of passive, aggressive, or assertive behavior. If you label the response as either passive or aggressive, write an assertive response.

1. **Situation:** There is one member of your project team who often interrupts you when you are speaking. You say: "You interrupt all of the time. Could you just hold on a minute?" _____
   Assertive response: _____

2. **Situation:** Your boss turns silent during a meeting with you and doesn't say what is on her mind. You say nothing about her silence. Instead, you rush on to finish what you are saying so that you can get out of her office. _____
   Assertive response: _____

3. **Situation:** You believe that you deserve a raise, but instead of seeing your supervisor about it you grumble about the large salaries of top management to your colleagues. _____
   Assertive response: _____

4. **Situation:** A joint management-union committee has been established to review the past year's safety performance. The

time of the meeting is convenient for others but not for you. You know you will not be able to attend regularly. You say: "I would like to be part of this committee, but the meeting time will not work with my schedule. What other times would be convenient for all of us?"_____
Assertive response: _____.

5. **Situation:** An employee is making a lot of mistakes in his work lately. You say: "I've noticed that the quality of your work has dropped in the past two weeks. I'd like to know if you agree and what you want to do about it." _____
Assertive response: _____

Here are potential answers.

1. **Aggressive.** Your goal may be to avoid interruptions while you are speaking. An assertive response is to say, "Excuse me, I would like to finish what I was saying and then you can give your comments."

2. **Passive.** One of your goals in this situation is to ensure that your boss is supportive of your position. If so, she needs to be encouraged to say what is on her mind rather than to remain silent. An assertive response might be for you to stop your presentation and say, "I've noticed that you haven't asked me many questions. Are there any questions or concerns that you want to express?"

3. **Passive.** Your goal may be to ask for a raise. If so, it is most direct to speak to your supervisor with prepared comments for why a raise is deserved. One assertive action is to schedule a meeting with your supervisor and initiate conversation by saying, "I'd like to discuss my performance and the potential of a raise with you."

4. **Assertive.** The goal of the situation is to contribute to the committee at a time that is convenient for all members.

5. **Assertive.** Your goal is to improve the quality of the employee's work.

. . . .

Additionally, make sure you identify the *real* issue. How often have you complained about one thing when something else really was bothering you? Television situation comedies use this theme for laughs, but in real life it can lead to major problems in both professional and personal relationships. You might have an assertive message that sounds correct, but if you are not expressing the real issue, communication is blocked. For example, to complain about someone's tardiness when the real issue is work left incomplete leaves the real issue unresolved.

The second part of the assertive message deals with feelings that sometimes are difficult to describe. However, not discussing feelings can block honest communication. Expressing your feelings about how the behavior affects your needs and your goals provides additional information for those who work with you. Try identifying your true feelings; don't overstate or understate them. A colleague who tends toward the dramatic indicates that "something awful has happened" when the copier breaks down. On the other hand, a more stoic friend indicates that she is "unhappy" when she is laid off from her job. Neither expression of feeling seems appropriate for the event.

It's also crucial that your message is heard by the person who has the power to take action to resolve your concern. Asserting to anyone else will only sound like a complaint—and it also wastes time and energy that could be applied to correcting the situation.

The third component of the assertive message is to express the consequences of the behavior in question. Whether positive or negative, explaining the consequences provides a listener with more complete information. Understanding the consequences and how the behavior affects you may encourage your listener to adjust in a way that benefits you. Consider the example of establishing a mutually convenient meeting time for committee members. It is helpful for participants to understand the consequence of changing the meeting time: that the group will meet its goal of having input from each committee member. Knowing the consequences provides useful information as decisions are made.

How would you handle the following situations in an assertive way?

1. Your boss keeps adding projects to your workload. You'd like to discuss the situation. You say:

---

2. You are finding that several employees often come to you with work that you have assigned them to do. Although you don't mind assisting when needed, you believe that they could do a better job of researching and problem solving. What do you do?

_____

_____

3. Your office is shared with a coworker. Both of you need frequent use of the computer, and you are having scheduling problems. Both of you seem to want to use it at the same time. What do you say?

_____

_____

Here are sample responses to each of the three situations:

1. "Suzanne, I would like to discuss my workload with you. As you probably know, I have a pretty full agenda, and I'd like to be sure that you and I are in agreement about my priorities. If not, I want to make the needed changes now."

2. "I don't mind assisting you if you have a specific question or concern. However, before you schedule time with me, please identify the purpose of the meeting, prepare to tell me of your progress to date in three to five minutes, and be specific in asking for my assistance. Keep in mind that this is your project; you are the project head. I expect to provide only a consulting perspective."

3. "John, I feel pretty frustrated about our scheduling conflicts over the use of the computer. We both seem to need it at the same time. Let's meet for an hour this afternoon to see if we can work this out. I'll bring some of my ideas, and it would help if you would bring some of yours. This must be pretty frustrating for you, too, and I'd like to see the situation resolved for both of us."

Assertiveness is a skill that requires regular attention and practice for effective use. Although each of us makes choices about how and when we use this behavior, we build credibility when assertiveness is used consistently. Most people recognize respectful and honest communication as a strength. It is likely that your ability to reach your goals will dramatically improve if you "grow" your assertiveness skill. Treating others with dignity and respect is a gift they deserve; treating yourself with dignity and respect is a gift you give yourself.

. . . .

BENEFITS OF ASSERTION

- Assertive communication increases self-confidence.
- Assertive communication reduces conflict.
- Assertive communication demonstrates consideration and respectful behavior.
- Assertive communication reduces stress.

. . . .

CHAPTER 5

CHANGING PEOPLE'S BEHAVIOR

E ffective goal setting is a key component to changing behavior—yours as well as others. When you ask someone to do something, you establish a goal for that person. And by setting a goal, you expect that person to behave in ways that lead to reaching that goal.

There are times when your goals mesh with the goals of others. But other times you will want to convince people to do something that you want done. What can you do to motivate others to work toward the goals you have set? How can you encourage others to understand your perspective? What can you do to change someone's behavior?

DEFINING BEHAVIOR

Since we emphasize behavior here, let's first define the word. For this discussion, *behavior* is a person's actions that are observable and that have a beginning and an end. However, your evaluation of someone's behavior often is biased by your experiences, judgments, and/or perceptions. A fair approach to evaluating behavior is to determine what specific results you want to see and observe those behaviors that lead to those results.

Examples of *nonbehavior*—or actions that cannot be measured and observed objectively in and of themselves—are courteousness, aggressiveness, neatness, and cheerfulness. What is judged as courteous by you may differ from what is viewed by one of your colleagues. What strikes you as cheerful may be seen as aloof by your supervisor. How about the employee who rarely smiles? You might judge him as unfriendly simply because he is not a smiler. However, in getting to know him, you discover that he does smile and does behave in a friendly manner as he becomes more comfortable in the relationship. There is the realization that perhaps he is a shy person, not unfriendly.

Before making judgments about the behavior of others, ask yourself the following questions:

■ Am I making a quick judgment based on my past experiences, feelings, and perceptions?

■ Am I looking for specific behavior on which to evaluate this person?

■ Am I defining behavior by making observations that are measurable, observable, and time-bound (with a beginning and an end)?

. . . .

Examples of behaviors that are measurable, observable, and time-bound are:

■ Completing paperwork correctly

■ Thanking an employee

■ Arriving at work by 8:00 A.M.

■ Shouting at a coworker

■ Giving step-by-step work instructions

. . . .

UNDERSTANDING BEHAVIOR

Regardless of who we are, our actions are in response to a variety of motivations. Understand this, and you will understand human behavior. Use the following principles, and you will strengthen your ability to reach your goals through the efforts of others.

Your Behavior Affects the Way Others Behave

To change someone else's behavior, you may first have to change your own. See the example on page 47.

A Person Behaves in Ways That Seem Reasonable to That Person

In order to change behavior, you need first to accept that any behavior is rational and logical to the person exhibiting it because his or her goals may differ from yours. Additionally, each one of us behaves in ways that are based on our unique backgrounds and experiences. Thus, we frequently respond to what seems to be the same situation in different ways. For example, while working at a nuclear power plant in New York, an engineer heard a lot of talk about radiation and the need to limit exposure to it. The plant had a policy that stated a specific level of radiation exposure above which no employee of the plant should experience. Although most employees were sensitive to this issue and were committed to following the policy, there was one group that did not.

Which of the following phrases is a behavior? Mark them with a *B*. Identify all nonbehaviors with an *N*.

1. Being rude _____
2. Picking someone up at 8:00 A.M. _____
3. Teaching a software package to a colleague _____
4. Seeking extra project assignments _____
5. Having an attitude problem _____
6. Being fairer to one work group than to another _____
7. Facilitating a meeting _____
8. Giving a good performance appraisal _____
9. Conducting a thirty-minute performance appraisal _____

     Answers: 1. N
                  2. B
                  3. B
                  4. B
                  5. N
                  6. N
                  7. B
                  8. N
                  9. B

To some of the foremen, exceeding this level of exposure developed into a contest—behavior that probably would not seem rational to the outside observer. But it made sense to the foremen. Part of the culture of their group was to exceed the exposure limit in order to prove to their peers how "macho" they were.

. . . .

A manager had an employee who was chronically late for work. She tried several techniques for handling the situation—anger, jokes, silent treatment. One day, she realized that her "counseling" was filled with idle threats regarding the lateness. She needed to change and be more specific, and directly communicate a goal to the employee. She needed to establish a specific goal, describe the consequences of not reaching that goal, and then follow through with the consequences. And so she arranged a meeting with the employee and said, "I have been angry about your tardiness for several months and we have discussed it frequently. This is our final discussion before I take action. One of your goals is to report to work on time. This meeting constitutes a formal warning regarding your tardiness. The next time you are late, a note will be put into your file. If there is a next time after that, you will be suspended for three days without pay. For the next six months, on the basis of your past record, action against your tardiness will be taken regardless of the circumstances."

. . . .

If a Behavior Leads to Positive Results, It Continues

When motivating employees to change their behavior, remember that positive consequences to any behavior will encourage that behavior, and negative consequences to any behavior are likely to diminish it. The catch is that the consequences must be perceived as positive or negative from the employees' points of view. Too often, supervisors implement consequences that are positive or negative from their points of view and then wonder why the behavior change did not take place. For example, an ongoing issue in manufacturing is the goal of improved safety. In this area, a primary concern is how to motivate employees to wear their safety hats and glasses. The dilemma is that employees perceive more positive consequences for not complying with the policy of safety gear than they do for adhering to it. It is easier, more comfortable, and more convenient to work without hard hat and glasses, so employees avoid them. The supervisory challenge is to motivate employees so that the positive consequences for compliance outweigh the positive consequences for noncompliance.

. . . .

In explaining the concept of rewards for positive behavior, people sometimes ask about *manipulation*. This word suggests a covert activity, qualities not included in this behavior principle. It's human nature to be interested in self-preservation. But we have needs, desires, and goals that can be met only with the assistance of others. Influencing the behavior of others based on what is pleasing to them and yourself as well is a win-win situation, not manipulation.

. . . .

Consequences That Are Immediate, Personal, and Guaranteed Have Greater Impact Than Those That Come After the Fact

The boss who says, "If you make three $500 sales this week, I'll guarantee you a bonus of $150 to be paid on Friday" motivates the employee more than the boss who says, "If you make some sales this week, maybe I can talk to the general manager about some sort of bonus for our sales team." On either a conscious or a subconscious level, we assess information to see how it benefits or hinders us. If we recognize the specific benefits of a consequence, then we are more likely to respond with the desired behavior.

The Consequences of Behavior Come From a Variety of Sources

The consequences of behavior can come from a boss, colleagues, subordinates, friends, and the organizational system. They can even come from the job itself. Unfortunately, this makes changing individual behavior difficult. Since there are many sources of consequences, understanding which have the greatest impact on the behavior you want to influence is essential. Frequently, you must work with the person whose behavior you are trying to change in order to discover these.

REINFORCING BEHAVIOR

Rewarding or reinforcing desired behavior is essential if you want a behavior to continue. Do you have a habit of telling others when and why you appreciate them? If you do, you probably are achieving more of your goals than those who don't. There are several ways that you can improve your ability to reinforce positive behavior:

■ **When people do a good job of reaching a goal, make certain they hear about it.** Employees want to know when they have done well, so talk to your employees when they do a good job. However, also reinforce behavior when something is done better than before. Managers have been heard to say, "I don't need to tell my people that they are doing a good job. They know they are if I'm not chewing them out for something." There is lively discussion when employees are asked if they get enough positive feedback. Usually no more than 10 percent in a group feel they receive adequate positive feedback for a job well done. Most people report that they get far more criticism than positive feedback. What they would like to hear is a sincere compliment when they are doing a good job and reaching desired goals.

. . . .

While providing training at a nuclear power plant a few years ago, one of the foremen commented, "You know, one 'aw shucks' knocks out ten 'attaboys.'" Others nodded in agreement. He continued by saying, "And we don't get enough 'attaboys' to have ten knocked out. Most of us need to be more positive, and we need to hear more positive words." His remarks underscore the importance of positive feedback as motivation for working toward goals. When we are doing a good job, most of us want to hear about it.

. . . .

In addition, outstanding performers as well as those who need improvement seek positive feedback. Contrary to some thinking,

outstanding performers can be motivated to even higher performance when they know what they do well as well as what they can
improve. Additionally, in knowing what they do well, outstanding
performers can then educate others to higher standards of performance. Using a performance rating of one through seven, with
seven indicating outstanding performance, managers often say, "I
never give a seven; no one is perfect." Your response can be, "A
seven does not equate with *perfect* performance; it is outstanding
performance. And outstanding performers deserve to be recognized." Managers may then argue, "But if you give a seven, employees won't be motivated to try harder." This always has been a weak
argument. Outstanding performers generally are motivated to do
even better when their performance is exemplary. Not recognizing
their performance is a demotivator.

Employees are better able to hear and respond to constructive
criticism when there is a balance of criticism and praise. If an employee hears only the negative, then there is little motivation to
improve. The thinking becomes, "Why bother?" Generally, employees want to do a good job and contribute to the organization. Providing feedback, both positive and negative, helps create an
atmosphere for improved performance toward established goals.

How often do you take the time to praise others for a job well
done?

_____

_____

Do you make a point of providing positive feedback to those who
help you accomplish your goals? How frequently?

_____

_____

■ **Reward desired behavior immediately after it occurs.**
When you reward desired behavior without delay, it has the greatest impact. Your employee is made aware that the reward is the
consequence of a particular behavior. His or her attention is then
focused on that behavior and its consequence. A colleague who
recently switched jobs from one corporate giant to another provides an example. He gave his first major presentation to key mem-

bers of the corporate staff. Following the presentation, the CEO and his supervisor immediately congratulated him on the presentation. His reaction was one of pleased surprise. At his previous position, his boss might say "good job" sometime following a presentation, but he couldn't count on it and the compliment was often stated in general terms. After experiencing the genuine and timely compliment, he commented, "It sure does help to know what your boss likes."

■ **Reinforce the small successes.** Often we wait until employees reach the big goal before we offer meaningful praise. Instead, divide a large goal into several smaller ones so that the intermediate goals seem more achievable, then offer reinforcement along the way. Most of us appreciate periodic reinforcement—it helps motivate us to continue our efforts. When we see the smaller successes accumulated, the momentum and energy build for reaching the final goal. Sincere praise also builds an improved relationship. So look for people who are doing things right. Take a proactive stance and look for successes to reinforce.

■ **Be specific in your praise.** Using assertive words, state the behavior that you liked, how you felt about it, and the consequences of that behavior. For example, note the difference between, "Corby, that was a good presentation" and "Corby, I liked your presentation; it was clear, concise, and well-prepared. I think your ideas will make a difference in the way the engineering manager makes her decision." And finally, affirm the person with a smile or handshake. Your personal warmth often strengthens the reinforcement.

Reinforcing behavior is part of an effective management style. In fact, this is part of the theory of Management by Walking Around (MBWA). One merit of this management style is that you have an opportunity to be on the floor, observing people. It's a rich opportunity to reinforce desirable behavior and correct undesirable behavior.

REINFORCING STATEMENTS

■ Thank you for taking the initiative. . . .
■ I appreciate your creativity. You enlivened that presentation.

- Your appraisal of that assistant was firm but fair.
- Your writing is clear and concise. It is easy to follow.
- Your efforts to increase efficiency have reduced the workload for all of us.

. . . .

. . . .

POSITIVE FEEDBACK

Suppose last week, you and your staff were responsible for completing a major project. One of your most talented and efficient employees was gone four of the five days, owing to illness. Although he had his own deadlines to meet, another staff member pitched in to help you meet your deadline. Your colleague's cooperation was helpful. What is the positive feedback that you want to give?

. . . .

CORRECTING BEHAVIOR

For many of us, criticizing what someone else has done comes fairly easily. But effectively correcting behavior takes energy and skill. In fact, correctly identifying the need to correct behavior is a first step. Often, an employee is unable to do as you say or reach a particular goal because he or she is not ready to accomplish the task for one of the following reasons: (1) the goal is not clearly stated; (2) adequate training or instruction is not provided; or (3) adequate resources (time, equipment, information) are not available. If you do not provide the needed instruction, skill, or resources for employees to accomplish their goals, then it is your responsibility to remedy that situation. However, if the problem is that an employee is not willing to work toward a goal, then you need to correct individual behavior. Effectively correcting that behavior involves several of the methods also discussed for reinforcing behavior.

■ Recognize that correction is part of the feedback process. This is a necessary and desired part of communication. Most of us want to do well in our work. Effective job performance feedback means hearing when we are doing well (reinforcement) and also hearing when our performance needs improvement (correction).

Managers need to provide this feedback for employees and for each other.

■ **Correction should occur as soon as possible, but in private.** Each of us has the right to know what we are doing wrong and why, so that we can take steps to improve performance. When correcting employee performance, describe the error specifically, tell what needs to be done differently, and explain why. Although correcting behavior needs to occur as soon as possible following the error, it should be done in private whenever possible. Your intent is to correct for improved performance. If you embarrass, anger, or humiliate an employee, you will lose ground in terms of the relationship as well as performance.

■ **When correcting, provide specific feedback.** Use assertive messages and listen carefully. For example, you might say, "I am disappointed that you did not seem prepared for this morning's presentation. Your main points were unclear and your overheads were not relevant to what you were saying. As you know, our goal was to provide the engineering manager with clear, relevant information to aid his budgeting decision for the waste incineration." When providing feedback, express the error and your feelings about it and explain the consequences of that error.

■ **Focus on the error, not the person.** Remember that it is the error (the behavior) that needs correction; the person is still of value to you. When possible, invite input from the individual who has made the mistake. In the previous example, you could ask, "What happened?" or "What can you do to prevent this from happening again?" or "What can you do to remedy this situation?"

Taking the time to ask an individual for input can provide helpful information as to why the error occurred and can help you design steps to prevent it from reoccurring. Asking for input also affirms that you see the employee as a person of value who can contribute to remedying the error. In this way, a learning opportunity emerges from the correcting process.

■ **Avoid holding grudges.** The correction process is one of moving forward, not of rehashing old mistakes and holding grudges. Doing so only wastes the precious resources of time, energy, and self-esteem. Develop the personal discipline to forgive mistakes.

You want to correct behavior so that progress toward your goals can continue. These techniques are essential if you want to minimize the frequency and impact of errors. No one is perfect and errors will occur. However, one measure of your effectiveness in motivating employees is the manner in which you correct their mistakes. Effective correction strengthens your authority and the respect that others have for you.

. . . .

You are the department head for an administrative group that sometimes experiences bottlenecks as a result of all the paperwork that must be completed. As a result, there are instances of paperwork being completed incorrectly, late, or not at all. To remedy the situation, you have tried yelling, threatening, and publicly denouncing the offenders during staff meetings. You realize that a new approach is warranted. How could you more constructively handle the situation to correct the problem with the paperwork?

. . . .

. . . .

TECHNIQUES TO AVOID WHEN CORRECTING BEHAVIOR

- Losing your temper
- Sarcasm
- Yelling
- Profanity
- Public reprimands
- Threats
- Humiliation
- Inconsistent actions

. . . .

PART III

3

EFFECTIVE GOAL SETTING AND MANAGEMENT SKILLS

CHAPTER 6

SETTING PRIORITIES

———————

B y now you probably have set specific goals for your work, and you have some ideas for accomplishing them. But how do you decide what to do first? A measure of your effectiveness is how skillfully you are able to establish your priorities in order to progress toward your goals. With many responsibilities and activities demanding your attention, you need a way to determine which goals receive the investment of your time and your energy. Only with a practical system for setting priorities will you be able to concentrate on the tasks for reaching your goals. Take a few moments to respond to the priority-setting checklist.

PRIORITY-SETTING CHECKLIST

	Yes	No
1. I set priorities regularly.	———	———
2. I establish priorities on a long-term basis as well as on a short-term basis.	———	———
3. I use criteria to establish my priorities.	———	———
4. I regularly work on the high-priority issues.	———	———

5. I recognize the value of applying my time and energy   _____ _____
   to the high-priority issues.
6. I communicate my priorities to others who are affected   _____ _____
   by my actions.

. . . .

A health-care executive faced with many interruptions in the day
established a quiet time for himself when he would address priorities. He learned to post a DO NOT DISTURB note on his office
door from 7:00 to 9:00 A.M. He then would concentrate on his
high-priority tasks, one at a time. The result has been an increas-
ing rate of productivity.

. . . .

SETTING YOUR PRIORITIES

How do you decide what to do each day? And how do you decide
which activities get your attention first? Often we set our priorities
in a way that feels comfortable to us rather than in a way that ad-
dresses our goals most effectively. Read these statements and check
those that apply to you:
I set my priorities by:

❑ My job description—"I first do what is related to my job."
❑ The squeaky wheel—"Whoever or whatever squeaks the
    loudest gets my attention."
❑ What my supervisor says to do.
❑ Doing the easy ones first—getting the minor tasks out of the
    way.
❑ Doing the most difficult ones first.
❑ Last in, first out—the latest issue gets the top priority.
❑ First in, first out—issues are dealt with in the order in which
    they come.
❑ What is most interesting at the moment.

None of these approaches is optimally effective because none
uses a rational, consistent criterion for determining what needs to

be done. And without rational criteria to set priorities, you may not work on your most important goals first.

. . . .

DOING FIRST THINGS FIRST

Problem: You return to your office and find ten telephone messages, and you have only thirty minutes in which to return the calls. **Solution:** Rank the calls in order of importance so you make the high-impact calls first.

. . . .

A rational system evaluates facts, is easy to use, can incorporate flexible criteria, and is accurate. Remember the 80-20 rule: Of all the things you could be doing to reach your goals, it is likely that about 20 percent of your current effort yields 80 percent of your results. So, there is a good reason to work smarter.

SETTING CRITERIA

An effective method for establishing priorities is to use a table (see Figure 6-1). The first column identifies your concerns, which may include your goals, current projects, and activities. Subsequent columns identify criteria to evaluate your concerns.

Criteria often used to rank concerns are *importance* and *urgency*. With regard to importance, consider the impact of each concern on your goals. Is it an activity of high impact? What impact is likely in terms of cost? Use of resources? What kind of an effect will this activity have on your reaching your goals? As you evaluate your

FIGURE 6-1.   TABLE FOR EVALUATING CONCERNS BY
RATING THE CRITERIA.

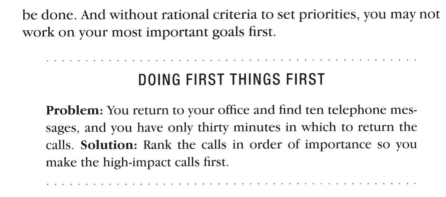

Concerns	Criteria	
	Importance	Urgency
1.		
2.		
3.		
4.		
5.		

activities using each criterion, assign a number to indicate the level of importance (high = 3, medium = 2, low = 1) and enter this number in the appropriate space of the table.

Follow the same guidelines for evaluating the urgency of a concern. What are its deadlines? Is it a project or goal that requires immediate attention, can it wait for a while, or can it be put aside indefinitely? As you did with the level of importance, assign a number value to indicate the level of urgency for each concern.

There are several thoughts to keep in mind as you use this table. First, people often equate urgency with importance. But the distinction is that importance has to do with *impact* and urgency has to do with *time*. Also, remember that each criterion is evaluated on its own merit. As you consider your activities and goals, evaluate their importance and then their urgency relative to each other, considering one concern at a time. For ease, focus, and consistency, limit your criteria to four.

The table in Figure 6-2 illustrates the method of using criteria to evaluate a list of goals, activities, and/or projects.

Rarely are there right and wrong answers, but this method of setting priorities is a defensible systematic strategy for establishing priorities. Once you identify the priority of your activities, you are poised to apply your time and energy to your goals more effectively. Your productivity will skyrocket!

Use this method when establishing both individual and group priorities. Even though you are likely to find that your priorities differ from those of others on your team, a systematic review of priorities provides a base of rational thought for supporting your position. When using this method, changes in opinion tend to be driven by facts rather than emotions. Generally you will find reaching agreement quicker and easier through a system that is rationally defensible.

To practice setting priorities, consider the issues, activities, and/or projects that you must deal with in the next week. Using the table shown in Figure 6-3 on page 62, list your issues and concerns, then rank each using the criterion of importance, then of urgency. Total the score and rank your results.

When establishing your criteria, you may decide to use different ones from importance or urgency. The criteria may change depending on what is most relevant to your goals. A key factor in setting priorities successfully is that you are consistent in choosing and applying the criteria.

FIGURE 6-2.   SAMPLE FILLED-OUT TABLE SHOWING THE CRITERIA RATING METHOD.

Activities	Criteria		Total	Ranking
	Importance	Urgency		
1. You have twenty-four hours to submit a grant proposal.	L = 1	H = 3	4	4
2. There has been an oil spill.	H = 3	H = 3	6	1
3. There is a formal complaint against one of your employees regarding sexual harassment.	M = 2	L = 1	3	7
4. A secretary needs to be hired within thirty days.	M = 2	H = 3	5	3
5. A time-and-motion study of the productivity in your department must be completed.	L = 1	L = 1	2	8
6. Four of your employees must attend training on sexual harassment two weeks from now.	M = 2	M = 2	4	5
7. Your CEO will be visiting your plant in one week to tour. His current priorities include adherence to environmental regulations.	H = 3	H = 3	6	2
8. Six performance appraisals must be completed in the next two months.	M = 2	M = 2	4	6

. . . .

A group of twenty department heads from a utility company identified twenty-five barriers that were keeping them from working together effectively. They needed to build consensus regarding their five most important issues. The criteria to prioritize each issue was the degree to which each issue: (1) met organizational goals, (2) enabled the productivity of each department head, and (3) enhanced communication of the group. Within three hours the group arrived at a common priority ranking for those issues and initiated planning to address the top concerns.

. . . .

FIGURE 6-3.   TABLE FOR RANKING ISSUES ACCORDING TO CRITERIA RATING.

	Criteria			
Issues	Importance	Urgency	Total	Ranking
1.				
2.				
3.				
4.				
5.				

YOUR PRIORITIES—DON'T KEEP THEM A SECRET!

A common complaint among employees is that the supervisors do not communicate their priorities. Instead, they assign work and establish goals with little or no apparent rationale. If you take the time to communicate your priorities in relationship to your goals, employees will better understand their role in helping you reach those goals. And your bonus is an improvement in morale!

CHAPTER 7

PLANNING

W ithout a plan, reaching your goals tends to be a hit-or-miss proposition, and time is easily wasted. Without a plan, you may find yourself reacting to the demands of others rather than focusing on your own goals. Without a plan, you will miss the benefits that come from using effective planning skills. Before considering the benefits of effective planning, perform the self-audit on the next page, and identify your strengths and areas for improvement with regard to planning.

The benefits of effective planning are many. For one, planning leads to higher productivity. Because a plan identifies what needs to be done, by when, and by whom, employees understand their role in accomplishing a specific goal. Arguments over responsibilities, resources, and work schedules diminish. As a result, there are fewer interruptions—employees have the information they need to do their jobs, so they can leave you alone to do yours.

There is also an improved use of resources. With employees understanding their part in reaching a goal, there is less overlap of effort and less time spent in confusion. Consequently, more time and energy are applied to getting results. A fourth benefit is the ability to delegate effectively. With a plan in place to reach your goals, you can identify the tasks to be delegated and the people who can complete them.

It is likely that your employees will enjoy improved morale as a result of your improved planning. Employees appreciate being given a focus, and they appreciate contributing to significant results. Too often, a lack of planning leads to frequent crisis management. And crisis management, with its frantic nature, often contributes to a mismanagement of resources including employees, which leads to a decline in morale. But, in contrast, better planning leads to improved quality. The quality problems that come from rushed or incomplete work are avoided. Systematic planning also helps to identify deviations from what should be occurring, so that you can make corrections before a crisis occurs.

PLANNING SELF-AUDIT

1. How many hours do you spend planning your daily, weekly, or monthly work? Daily _____ Weekly _____ Monthly _____

2. Do you have a plan for reaching your goals? Yes _____ No _____

3. How many hours are spent managing crises on a daily basis? _____

4. Could some of these crises be averted with planning? Yes _____ No _____

5. Do you have plans or policies to manage the most frequent concerns and tasks in your department? Yes _____ No _____

6. Do you set clear goals for yourself? For your employees? (Self) Yes _____ No _____ (Employees) Yes _____ No _____

7. Do you encourage the use of a systematic planning process when trying to reach significant goals? Yes _____ No _____

8. Do you remember to evaluate your plan in terms of what can go wrong? Yes _____ No _____

9. Do you have the skills to plan effectively? Yes _____ No _____

Take a moment to consider your current work situation. What are three benefits of planning that could accrue to you?

1. _____

2. _____

3. _____

PLANNING IS A MANAGEMENT SKILL

Many managers find they become less reactive and more proactive as they increasingly practice effective planning. Instead of embracing a management style that reacts to the crises of the day, planners plan their tomorrows. In the shift from a reactive to a proactive stance, managers find that the number of brushfires they must fight decreases. They anticipate problems and have a plan in place to handle them calmly and systematically.

Planning will help you identify the steps necessary for reaching your goals. In contrast, failing to plan can lead to the perception that you are an ineffective manager. You'll attain fewer results and waste resources because of a lack of planning.

Additionally, conflicts among employees increase because of the confusion that surrounds their jobs. Who is supposed to do what? By when? And for what reason? These are the questions you hear when employees do not have a plan to guide them.

Two additional problems that occur when there isn't sufficient planning are the increased probability of accidents and higher production costs. Inadequate staffing, tight schedules, a lack of resources, and increased time pressures contribute to that higher risk environment. And higher production costs accrue as a result of reduced output, lower morale, and higher stress levels.

Many managers claim that they have no time to plan. Day-to-day events and activities push regular planning into the background. And it's true that fighting brushfires takes time and energy away from fire prevention. However, planning saves time in the long run. Numerous experiments have been made to measure the value of planning. One group applies more time to planning, while a second group goes about business as usual. Repeatedly, the planned work is completed more quickly and with higher-quality results.

Front-line supervisors in a paper mill repeatedly stated that their workload was overwhelming, and that they had no time for planning. The classic response was, "We're too busy fighting fires to plan." Challenged to spend just twenty minutes a day planning, several of the supervisors agreed to give it a try. Within four weeks, those who planned their days found that they were facing fewer production crises and fewer employee conflicts. They also reported feeling more confident about their ability to do their job.

KEY PLANNING STEPS

Six basic questions frame the planning process: Who? What? When? Where? Why? How? Answering these six questions is essential to effective planning. *Who* determines responsibility. It identifies the person responsible for completing each part of the plan. Knowing this enhances teamwork and personal accountability for accomplishing tasks. *What* establishes the goal and details the results and standards to be met. For example, "Make six widgets" is a goal. But natural questions are, "Can you be more specific?" and "How long do we have to make them?" If you can be more specific, say so. "Make six four-sided blue widgets within the next seven days" is a focused goal. The more specific your goal, the more specific your plan can be. And the clarity of your plan helps diminish confusion, increase confidence, and contribute to the effective use of resources.

When marks the time frame for the plan's beginning and end, as well as providing scheduled progress checks along the way. So for each step, identify the time allotted for completing that step. *Where* identifies the place for carrying out the steps of the plan. *How* defines the steps to be completed, and within each step, clarifies the procedures to be used. Finally, *why* provides the personal motivation of those involved to work the plan and to reach the goal. Remember that motivation differs depending on the people involved. Take the time to identify what motivates each of your employees to accomplish a particular goal, and then encourage them to use that information.

ENSURING A FAIL-SAFE PLAN

There are a few more ways you can maximize the benefits of your plan. One is to avoid making assumptions. Be specific—anticipate and answer questions, and document your plan and your progress. Another is to ensure that you look for potential problems in your plan. Parts of your plan are apt to be vulnerable, and these vulnerabilities could disrupt the success of your plan and jeopardize your ability to reach the goal.

For example, initiating something new creates a vulnerability. If you are doing something for the first time, all the kinks may not have been worked out. Tight deadlines create a vulnerable situation, and so do activities controlled by more than one person. In each situation, consider how you can minimize the potential difficulty.

A third suggestion is to ensure that you communicate with people whose cooperation is essential for the success of the plan. And these people sometimes are different from those who are responsible for carrying out the plan. You will also want to emphasize follow-up and follow-through. Your attention to detail will ensure that nothing falls between the cracks.

Finally, you need to establish a fair method for providing specific feedback to those working the plan, so that praise is given when warranted and correction is provided as needed.

CHAPTER 8

DELEGATING

Which of your responsibilities could be handled by someone else in your organization? How much of the work you do could be delegated to someone else? Of all the management skills that can have an impact on your effectiveness, delegation is one of the most important. The effective delegator enables achievement of greater results in others. When you delegate projects, you give others authority, responsibility, and accountability.

When you fail to delegate, however, two key problems arise:

1. You handle work that others could do more efficiently and at a lower cost to the organization.
2. You are not investing your time and resources in projects that only you are best prepared to do.

In effect, you waste valuable resources of time, money, morale, and energy.

Many managers do not feel comfortable delegating work, however. Delegation is a relatively easy concept to understand but is difficult to apply. What about you? Are you an effective delegator? Before reading further, consider your attitude and experience by taking the delegation self-audit on the next page.

If you answered "yes" to ten or more of the questions, then you are well prepared to delegate, and you probably are rarely accused of "dumping" on your direct reports. But if you responded "no" four or more times, then you are not yet an effective delegator. Developing your delegating skills will enhance your achievement of goals that require the effort and cooperation of others.

DELEGATING SELF-AUDIT

	Yes	No
1. Do you trust your staff to handle job assignments?	_____	_____
2. Do you avoid being a perfectionist?	_____	_____
3. Do you give job instructions effectively?	_____	_____
4. Do you believe that others can do a job as well as you can?	_____	_____
5. Do you enjoy managing work rather than doing the work?	_____	_____
6. Do you recognize that making mistakes is part of learning?	_____	_____
7. Do you follow up with people after delegating?	_____	_____
8. Do you appreciate the skills and talents of those who work for you?	_____	_____
9. Do you avoid crisis management?	_____	_____
10. When you delegate, do you leave your staff alone to do the work that you have assigned?	_____	_____
11. Do you recognize that delegation is sometimes done in increments rather than as an all-or-nothing proposition?	_____	_____
12. Do you support your direct reports by your feedback, your actions, and your loyalty?	_____	_____
13. Do you delegate to the lowest possible level in your organization?	_____	_____

STRATEGIES FOR BUILDING A DELEGATING ATTITUDE

The delegation self-audit had you consider some ideas that affect your attitude about delegating. Let's take a closer look at these ideas:

1. **Trust your staff.** If you do not trust one or more members of your staff, take time to consider why not. Is the person not trustworthy? Is the person incapable of handling work that you would like to delegate? Then ask yourself even deeper questions to probe the root cause of your lack of trust:

■ Have you provided adequate job instructions?

■ Have you provided adequate feedback (positive and negative) about your staff members' job performances?

■ Have you delegated authority as well as responsibility?

■ Do you provide support and build confidence in your people?

■ Do you encourage employees to seek you out when there is a question?

2. **Avoid seeking perfection.** That search is futile, and is the cause of misused and wasted resources. Resources applied to a "perfect" project are resources taken away from other projects of value. Instead of striving for perfection, establish a standard of quality and provide a time frame for reaching it. Then let your staff choose any reasonable means to reach that goal.

3. **Understand that giving effective job instructions is related to effective delegation practices.** When you delegate, you may need to provide instructions for completing the job successfully. Explain the assignment clearly, and establish controls for regular feedback. Ensure that your employee understands and accepts the job before assuming that it is delegated and off your desk.

4. **Recognize that others have the talent and ability to accept and complete assignments.** Sometimes managers do not delegate because they believe that they can complete assignments better than anyone else can. This belief often develops because an employee handles a job differently from the way a supervisor would. Handling the job differently doesn't mean that it is done better or worse, just differently. However, if you and your employee establish the goal to be achieved, the standards to uphold, and a time frame to follow, then the method—within reason—should not matter.

. . . .

The owner of a retail business once called in a consultant to improve the practical skills of a jewelry repairman who worked in the store. When asked about the problem, the owner said, "The problem is that he doesn't repair jewelry the same way that I do." The owner indicated that he trusted his employee, and that he had the skill to do the work, but that the employee had a different way of doing things. The consultant then asked the owner three questions: "Does your repairman complete the repair jobs to the customers' satisfaction? Are you impressed with the quality of his work? Does he complete his work on a timely basis?" When the store owner replied yes to these questions, the consultant said, "There isn't a problem with your employee. The problem is your being unable to leave him alone after you have delegated the job to him. The employee is meeting your goal within the required time, and he is satisfying your customers. It doesn't matter that he does the work in a different way than you do. What matters is that he gets the desired results."

5. **Recognize your true interests.** Delegation is difficult for some people because they prefer doing the work rather than managing it. Ironically, people often are promoted to management as a result of their technical excellence, rather than their ability to manage projects and people. If you know that you prefer doing the work rather than planning, organizing, delegating, and controlling a project, then make that known. You do not want to find yourself moved into an area where you must manage other people's work.

6. **Consider delegation a way to teach skills.** Employees are reluctant to accept a delegated responsibility when mistakes are more frequently punished than accepted as part of learning. Your willingness to accept mistakes affects the willingness of your staff to accept assignments. Employees must believe that they will be supported for their efforts, even if they do not achieve a goal and/or mistakes are made. The risk of not succeeding is minimized if your delegation is realistic, appropriate resources are provided, and the assignment is understood.

7. **Build in controls to follow up on progress once a project has been delegated.** Those to whom you delegate should be left alone to do the work, but checking on progress is a natural part of

management. Build in checkpoints to help identify potential problems so that they can be handled before they become major.

8. **Praise the efforts of your staff.** Praising people's efforts provides important feedback and often motivates continued effort. Your words of praise, a brief note, or a handshake express your appreciation for the skills and talents of your employees. An effective manager shares the spotlight easily and frequently.

. . . .

"Early in our company's history, when someone sold an order, we rang a bell. It quickly became a tradition. We looked forward to hearing the bell for ourselves and for others. It was a simple but effective way to indicate that people were doing a good job. Now that our company is much larger, we use a symbolic bell attached to an engraved walnut base. It is a traveling trophy that continues to symbolize our pride in our employees and their excellent work."—Frank Russell, President, Excellence in Training Corporation

. . . .

9. **Avoid crisis management.** Crisis management impedes delegation. When crises rule, time is not applied to planning, prioritizing, and delegating projects and work assignments related to your goals. When crisis management is at the forefront, delegating the work to reach significant goals takes a backseat. Avoid crisis management by adhering to established planning schedules and delegating your work.

10. **Avoid reverse delegation.** This situation occurs when an employee returns assigned work to the boss with the expectation that the boss will take it back uncompleted! Use effective delegation practices. Ask questions, expect answers, and assist employees to help ensure that they will complete the work assignments as expected.

11. **Do not use delegation as an all-or-nothing proposition.** Because of varying skills and confidence levels, work often needs to be delegated gradually. As an employee becomes more competent and confident, give him or her more authority with the accompanying accountability.

12. **Support your employees.** Provide the resources and assistance you would expect if you were completing the work assign-

ment yourself. When delegating, your job is to see that the work gets done. Communicate your expectations before the work begins, then tell employees what you expect and what support they can expect.

13. **Delegate to the lowest possible level.** You want to make the best possible use of resources, energy, and knowledge. For example, operating decisions often are best made by people responsible for day-to-day operations. They are the ones with readily available facts and applied experiences. Employees often can contribute to a better operating decision because they are closer to the situation. Delegation to the lowest possible level ensures that you apply your time to the efforts of your position, making you maximally effective.

These thirteen ideas can change your perspective on delegating to your staff. Take a few moments to consider your daily work schedule and then respond to the following questions.

- How many hours do you spend (on a daily basis) doing what others could do? _____
- What is the dollar cost of that time on a weekly basis? _____
- On an annual basis? _____
- If you delegate that work, what projects could you now handle to make more effective use of your time?

_____

_____

ACTION STEPS FOR IMPOROVED DELEGATING

Can you be a teacher? A coach? A cheerleader? If yes, then you can become a more effective delegator. Six action steps for improved delegating follow. Decide which steps will strengthen your delegation skills:

1. **Select a person whose judgment you trust.** You need to be willing to delegate the task to see the project to its completion. Selecting capable people who get results reflects well on your ability to set goals and make decisions.

2. **Invite input from your staff regarding their interest in and time for projects.** This increases their commitment to the

project. In contrast, delegating unilaterally tends to build resentment and discontent.

3. **Offer training when you delegate.** Understand that delegation has a learning curve. People to whom you delegate may need time to develop the knowledge and confidence to handle the task. Delegate at a pace that is fair to the abilities of your staff.

4. **Delegate projects and assignments that are enjoyable.** Don't just give out the tedious or difficult jobs. Employees quickly feel "dumped on" if only the less pleasant projects are delegated. Most of us understand that any job entails dirty work, but we want a reasonable balance.

5. **Delegate a whole project whenever possible.** If a project must be divided, ensure that team members understand how their work contributes to the whole. Without that understanding, they may feel as though they are working in a vacuum, and become less motivated.

6. **Establish your expectations for communication and feedback.** Encourage employee input. Provide follow-up without giving the feeling you are breathing down an employee's neck. Progress reports help keep everyone on track.

Read the statements that follow and then decide which of the six action steps just introduced is not being followed. Mark your answer by identifying the number of the action step in the space provided.

1. "Why did you add this project to my department? You've already given us enough work for six months. Most of us are working ten-hour days. Why didn't you talk to me before assigning this?" _____

2. "You gave this to me because you hate detail work. Well, I hate it too." _____

3. "This assignment requires drafting expertise. I don't have the background for this. It will take me twice as long to do this as it would take Suzanne." _____

4. "I thought you wanted me to take care of this. If you do, please give me a chance to get it done. We agreed that I would complete this assignment in seven days, but you've been checking on me once a day." _____

5. "I don't know what happened, either. I thought John was supposed to take care of that particular account. It's frustrating to know only bits and pieces about this project." _____

Answers:
1. 2   2. 4   3. 1   4. 6   5. 5

CHAPTER 9

TIME MANAGEMENT

D o you wish that there were more hours in a day? Do you frequently find yourself trying to catch up? Do you feel that time controls you more than you control it? Many of us cry that there is too little time to accomplish all that we would like to do. However, rather than having too little time, the issue may be the way you manage time.

There are strategies that can optimize your use of time so that you can spend more time working toward your goals. For example, ask yourself the following question regularly and thoughtfully: "What is the best use of my time right now with regard to my goals?" Often we function without considering how our time is spent. Questioning yourself about the best use of your time "right now" encourages you to stop and think. You can make a conscious decision about the value of what you are doing. If you plan your time so that you concentrate on those activities that relate to your goals, you raise the probability that you will reach your goals.

Take the time management self-assessment on the next page. Those statements to which you answer "no" are time-management red flags—areas that, when improved, contribute to more effective use of time.

USING A TIME LOG

How do you manage your time? Do you really know how your time is used? To determine your use of time, record your activities using a time log. Although keeping a running total of how you use the minutes in a day may not seem appealing initially, the information you'll get about yourself is worth the effort. The time log is a simple but valuable tool for learning more about how you use the hours in your day. When you understand where your time is really going, you can decide how best to invest your hours. Your time log can be a daily calendar divided into fifteen-minute units, or you can use the time log provided on page 77.

TIME MANAGEMENT SELF-ASSESSMENT

	Yes	No
1. My goals are written down in a specific, measurable way.	____	____
2. I know the results I want at work for the coming week.	____	____
3. I judge my results by accomplishment, not by level of activity.	____	____
4. I have a system in place to minimize unwanted mail.	____	____
5. I have an effective system in place for reviewing mail, memos, and paperwork.	____	____
6. I attend meetings only if I know the purpose, value, and my contribution to them.	____	____
7. I make it a practice to be prepared when attending meetings.	____	____
8. I look for ways to decrease wasted and unproductive time.	____	____
9. I make a habit of doing the things that need to be done in the right way to avoid mistakes and rework.	____	____
10. I establish time frames for getting my work done.	____	____
11. I use waiting time to get things done.	____	____
12. I can recognize a time waster and take steps to eliminate it.	____	____
13. I listen carefully to optimize communication.	____	____

Use a time log to track your activities for five business days. Then evaluate the results to find patterns and trends in how you use your time. Some people find that their effectiveness is hampered by interruptions; others are hampered by misguided priorities, an overload of paperwork, unclear assignments, or inefficient and ineffective meetings. Other insights come from the use of a time log. For instance, you may discover blocks of time to which you can apply efforts to accomplish your goals.

TIME LOG

Date _____

Time	Activity
6:00 A.M.	
6:30 A.M.	
7:00 A.M.	
7:30 A.M.	
8:00 A.M.	
8:30 A.M.	
9:00 A.M.	
9:30 A.M.	
10:00 A.M.	
10:30 A.M.	
11:00 A.M.	
11:30 A.M.	
12:00 P.M.	
12:30 P.M.	
1:00 P.M.	
1:30 P.M.	
2:00 P.M.	
2:30 P.M.	
3:00 P.M.	
3:30 P.M.	
4:00 P.M.	
4:30 P.M.	
5:00 P.M.	
5:30 P.M.	
6:00 P.M.	
6:30 P.M.	

PROCRASTINATION

Do you find that there are times when you haven't worked toward one of your goals? Are there some activities that you deliberately

avoid? One reason why time slips away is that we tend to procrastinate. Procrastination is the "ability" to put off until tomorrow what
could be accomplished today. Most of us are guilty of this at one
time or another. Unfortunately, over time we become adept at wel-
coming diversions and at avoiding what needs to be done.

Take a few moments to respond to the statements below.

I find that I procrastinate because:

	Yes	No
The task or project is overwhelming.	_____	_____
The task or project is difficult.	_____	_____
The task or project is time-consuming.	_____	_____
The task or project is unpleasant.	_____	_____
The task or project is effort-intensive.	_____	_____
The task or project is unrewarding.	_____	_____

Although it is unlikely that the tasks you dislike will go away,
you can change your behavior and meet the "procrastination challenge." Your self-discipline and the following strategies can help:

■ **Identify your motivation for getting started.** For example,
you could reward yourself for working for three hours. Or you
could remind yourself that the completion of this project will raise
your credibility in the eyes of your supervisor. Decide what motivates you and then follow through on it.

■ **Ensure that this task or project is a priority.** Use your
priority-setting skills to identify the value of work on this project. If
it is not a priority, eliminate it from your to-do list.

■ **Break the task or project into its component parts.** This
way it is more manageable. Begin by working on just one part of
the task.

■ **Accept that some projects require a lot of time.** Although
we often do not have long blocks of uninterrupted time, we can
schedule some time (as we would a meeting) and make some progress on the longer task.

■ **Use a ten-minute strategy.** You can commit ten minutes of
effort to almost any task. And ten minutes is enough to get you
started. If after ten minutes you feel that you must stop, then do.

But you may find that you want to keep going after the initial plunge.

■ **Reward your effort.** The minutes that you spend procrastinating can be applied to a reward if you just go ahead and take the plunge. The reward may be small, but it can have a high impact on performance. Remember one of the principles of human behavior: We continue to do those things that are rewarding; we stop doing those things that are not.

■ **Set deadlines for yourself and meet them.**

■ **Avoid absolutes.** Rarely is anything perfect or absolute. Imposing this pressure on yourself impedes progress.

INTERRUPTIONS

If you had a dollar for every time you allowed an interruption in your day, wouldn't you be well on your way to financial independence? Realize that many interruptions are a result of decisions that you make. And a decision to be interrupted may take time away from working on one of your goals. Each time you do not say no—that you pick up your telephone, open your door, or don't communicate that you are busy—you make a decision to be interrupted.

There are several strategies for controlling interruptions. First, refer to your time log and identify those interruptions that seem to occur on a regular basis. If an interruption will contribute to meeting your goal, schedule it to be dealt with at a particular time. More likely you can delegate it to a more appropriate source.

You can also group potential interruptions. For instance, instead of handling telephone calls through the day, have messages taken and then return calls at a designated time of day. To make your telephone calls more productive:

■ Avoid social conversation.

■ State the goal of the call.

■ Put a time limit on your calls.

■ Provide a time and number for reaching you if the person you are calling is not available.

■ Identify phrases you can use to end your calls politely.

Since another cause of interruption is an open office door, learn to control who steps through it. People who come in to see you generally view the interruption as important—perhaps even urgent. However, the interruption may interfere with activities related to your high-priority goals. Before deciding to accept a visitor, ask for the reason for (goal of) the visit and establish a time limit. If your visitor needs more than ten minutes, suggest a scheduled meeting. Here are five other actions you can take to minimize the impact of drop-in visitors:

1. Do not accept interruptions from people who can have their needs taken care of elsewhere.
2. Do not invite a drop-in visitor to sit down.
3. Do not accept interruptions during your quiet time—this is when you can make progress toward your goals.
4. Establish a policy of encouraging employees and colleagues to schedule appointments when possible.
5. Meet visitors outside of your office.

Consider the following ideas and mark the ones you would be willing to implement as of tomorrow:

■ Begin work fifteen to twenty minutes earlier than you usually do. Getting started even a few minutes early gives you time to mentally prepare for the day.

■ The night before, organize your work for the next day. Identify your priorities, get your desk ready, and think through the next day's accomplishments.

■ Be respectful and courteous of others' time. Limit the interruptions and visits you make to others.

■ Use a clock or a timer to keep you on track.

■ Concentrate on the task at hand. Each time an interruption takes place, you have to stop and then get started again. Efficiency and effectiveness increase when you schedule uninterrupted time for your work.

■ Learn to say no, but be willing to explain your rationale. Doing so saves time in the long run by avoiding assumptions, misunderstandings, and hurt feelings.

■ Plan for essential interruptions. Rarely are circumstances ideal, so build flexibility into your schedule.

■ During work hours, avoid the people who can usurp your time and stay away from places that steal your time.

■ Be assertive. Doing so encourages you to make your own choices and ensures that you communicate them fairly and respectfully.

Your time is precious. Time spent in unproductive or low-priority activities is a resource taken away from activities that achieve your goals. Managing your time more effectively can help you reach your goals more quickly and efficiently. There is no magic to learning to manage time. It is a simple matter of identifying how your time is currently used, identifying the habits that need to be changed, and applying the strategies to change those habits. The combination of dedication and perseverance, and the application of time-management strategies, will be your key to successful goal achievement.

PART IV

4

ACHIEVING YOUR GOALS

CHAPTER 10

GETTING HELP IN REACHING YOUR GOALS

B usiness goals often interweave the personal and the professional. If your goal is to get a raise, the best way to get that
raise may be to take on special projects, learn new skills, or
otherwise increase your benefit to your employer. If your goal is to
upgrade the IT infrastructure to cut long-term operating costs by
25 percent, your success may translate into an increase in status or
the likelihood of promotion.

These business goals almost always involve other people. Your
boss has to agree that you deserve a raise or the opportunity to take
on projects or training. Your boss may not be the final decision
maker; other managers often play a role. In the IT project, you
have a universe of stakeholders: customers, colleagues, suppliers,
subject matter experts, users, and more. Each has a certain power
or influence over your project and also has needs and wants.

Managing people is often the most difficult challenge of any
job. People seldom check their humanity at the door when they get
to work. They bring their personal as well as professional goals into
the office, whether we like it or not. The "unofficial organization"
is ultimately just as real as the official one, and you must work with
it constructively in order to achieve your goals.

UNDERSTANDING MOTIVATION

If someone isn't helping you to achieve your goals, there are three possible reasons:

1. **Ignorance**—They *don't know* what you want.
2. **Inability**—They *can't do* what you want.
3. **Choice**—They *won't do* what you want.

   1. **Ignorance.** If people don't know what you want, the problem isn't with them—it's with you. Even if you know you've told them, don't assume the message has really gotten across. You may not have been as clear as you could have been, and they may not have been listening as well as they might have. It's always a good idea to check to make sure people really do know what you want. If that is the only thing standing in the way of their action, you're done.

   2. **Inability.** When we say "can't do," it's a literal "can't do": if we offered a million-dollar bounty, nothing would change. "Can't do" situations can sometimes be fixed by training, by access to necessary resources, by going to a different person, or by altering your request. There is nothing personal here but merely a problem. You can fix it or you can't.

   3. **Choice.** If someone knows what you want and can do it, then he or she is able to make a choice about whether to do it. Why would the person choose not to do it? Again, three reasons:

1. Performance is punished.
2. Failure is rewarded.
3. Performance doesn't matter.

   Watch out for "perverse incentives"—ways in which we inadvertently push people in the direction of the very behavior we want them to avoid. If you get rewarded for doing a great job with even more work, perhaps that great job isn't completely in your own interest. If failure to exceed your quota for the month gets you better liked by your colleagues and does not provoke an adverse consequence from management, failure may give you the greatest personal reward. If you think no one reads or cares about that weekly report, it doesn't seem to matter much if you do it well or poorly.

When you're in a leadership role or simply need help and cooperation from your colleagues, try to find out *why* they're behaving as they do. If you know whether their behavior is a choice or not, you can pick the best strategy for getting results. Use the following assessment form to help you diagnose the situation:

BEHAVIORAL INCENTIVE TOOL

Name _____

Job _____

Date _____

What do you want this person to do?

_____

_____

What is the person doing instead?

_____

_____

Does the person know what you want him or her to do?   ____Yes ____No

If yes, describe why you believe the person knows.

_____

_____

Can the person do what you want him or her to do?   ____Yes ____No

If no, describe the problem.

_____

_____

How could you solve the problem—e.g., training, resources, change person, change request?

_____

_____

What are the consequences for the person if he or she does what you want?

_____

_____

Are these consequences harmful or undesirable to the person? If so, how?

_____

_____

How could you reduce the negative consequences to the other person of not doing what you want?

_____

_____

What are the consequences for the person if he or she doesn't do what you want?

_____

_____

Are these consequences beneficial to the person? If so, how?

_____

_____

How could you reduce the benefit to the other person of not doing what you want?

_____

_____

Does this situation or action matter to the person? If so, why?

_____

_____

How could you make the situation or action matter more?

_____

_____

UNDERSTANDING WIN-WIN NEGOTIATION

In *Getting to Yes,* Harvard negotiation experts Roger Fisher and William Ury tell the story of two sisters fighting over the last orange. They decided, sensibly enough, to compromise and share equally. They cut the orange in half and each sister took her piece. The first sister peeled her half of the orange and ate it, but the other sister was baking. She threw the fruit away but kept the peel, because she needed to grate it for her recipe.

Logic and common sense tell us that if you cut up an orange, all its pieces put together have to equal 100 percent. But this orange had the magic ability to be split 100-100 because *needs are not necessarily reciprocal.*

When you go to the store to buy something, you decide getting the merchandise is better than keeping your money. The store prefers to take your money rather than keep all its merchandise. Everybody's better off.

That's known as *win-win negotiation.* If I find something I don't particularly need but that you find valuable, I may be able to trade it for something you don't need but I do. Not only is there a much greater chance of reaching a deal in the first place, but there's also the highly desirable possibility that neither side has to lose.

The possibility of a win-win scenario is much more common than you may suppose. Frequently there's a "don't know" problem. People don't look, and so it's completely logical they don't see. We can't promise there's an available win-win in every single scenario, but you'll never know unless you look. Here are the factors to consider:

FINDING THE WIN-WIN SCENARIO

1. **Your Position.** Your position is what you're asking for. *Examples*: "I want a 10 percent raise." "I think we need to buy four new routers to handle increased Internet traffic."

_____

_____

2. **Your Interest.** Why do you want a raise? Is it the money, is it the opportunity, or is it to do more interesting work? Is a raise the best way to achieve your goals? How else can you satisfy your interest if you don't get a raise? Why do we need four new

routers for the IT department? What capacity or capability does that give us? Are there other ways to achieve those qualities?

_____

_____

3. **The Other Side's Position.** What they're asking for.

_____

_____

4. **Their Interest.** Why do they want to achieve their position? Can the underlying interests be resolved in other ways?

_____

_____

You can't negotiate *positions* with a win-win outcome. If our positions are in opposition, one will win and the other will lose, or both will give up some of what they want in a compromise. Instead, negotiate *interests.* What is your boss's interest (not yours) in giving you a raise? Well, your boss may want to keep you from going to the competition or may need to give you a new major project or may want you to keep up your high level of performance. If the organization gets more value from your increased role than the raise costs the company, both sides have won.

It's always worth the time and effort to look for a win-win solution. Even if a total win-win scenario slips through your grasp, often you can find at least some extra value to add for the other person, which can only make things better and easier.

CHAPTER 11

GETTING THE POWER TO GET THINGS DONE

I n Chapter 10 we learned about the role of motivation and negotiation in working with other people. Those are vital, but they
aren't always sufficient. We've talked about the "unofficial organization," and why it's not reasonable to expect people to leave all
personal desires and characteristics at home.

You can't explain everything about an organization if you only
pay attention to the official part. There is usually another factor at
work—office politics.

Office politics often have a big impact on whether you achieve
your goals. Unfortunately, most of us have a pretty negative view of
office politics. It seems as if there is a choice: You can be successful
or you can be ethical. Either way, it's a bad choice.

Even more important, it's also a false assumption. Most of the
time the politically smart choice is also what's in the organization's
best interest. It's politically smart to do high-quality work. It's politically smart to be seen as a polite, decent person. It's politically
smart to get a difficult project done.

To achieve any of your goals in the workplace, you'll need to
work within both the official and unofficial organizations. Working
with the unofficial organization is office politics.

Politics—whether international, local, or office—is about the
unofficial way in which resources get divided among competing

interests. To achieve your goals, you need certain resources. To get the resources, you need *power.*

This chapter is all about power. Talking about power often makes people uncomfortable. Isn't being power hungry a bad thing? Well, it depends. Is power often necessary to help you reach your goals? Absolutely.

Engineers define *power* as "energy that overcomes resistance to achieve work." The consequence of no power equals no work. But "power corrupts." Or does it?

Research says that petty power ("hall monitor" power) is the most corrupting. You don't have enough power to get anything done, but you have just enough to let you torture those under your thumb.

But power also seems self-centered. We recognize the people who look out for number one. We don't necessarily despise the person, but it's not the most attractive quality, either. And it's difficult to trust them to do anything outside their clear self-interest.

The essential ethical questions about power are:

1. How did you get it?
2. How are you using it?
3. What is your goal?

There are both ethical and unethical routes to power and influence. There's quid pro quo, or "this for that"—in other words, you scratch my back and I'll scratch yours. Doesn't sound very public-spirited, does it?

It all depends. If I promise not to rat you out about that phony expense report and in exchange you'll cover up the office supplies I stole, clearly there is an ethical problem. It's not the trading of favors that is the problem but the nature of the favors being traded.

If you do excellent work, does that give you more power? Maybe not as much as you think it should, but you usually get some more. If you help other people, they feel at least some obligation to help you in return. If you pick up new skills, you pick up more influence and more involvement.

Maybe you're thinking that you do all these things, but you don't get any extra power, you just get exploited. If so, it's likely the problem involves what you *don't* do. A lack of people skills can drain your power. It may be that you don't like being in your job, and your frustration and unhappiness are showing.

Power comes from many sources, as shown in the POWER

model (Figure 11-1). The sources of power reinforce each other: Respect power and relationships power reinforce one another if both are strong, but if one is weak, it siphons power from the other.

REASON POWER

At the core of the model is *Reason*, the reason you want the power in the first place. We talked earlier about the people who simply "look out for number one." If that's the reason and people know it, then other sources of power are made weak. If your reasons are considered more organizationally or socially appropriate, or if your power will end up helping others, your quest is considered more legitimate, and your power is strengthened.

FIGURE 11-1. THE POWER MODEL.

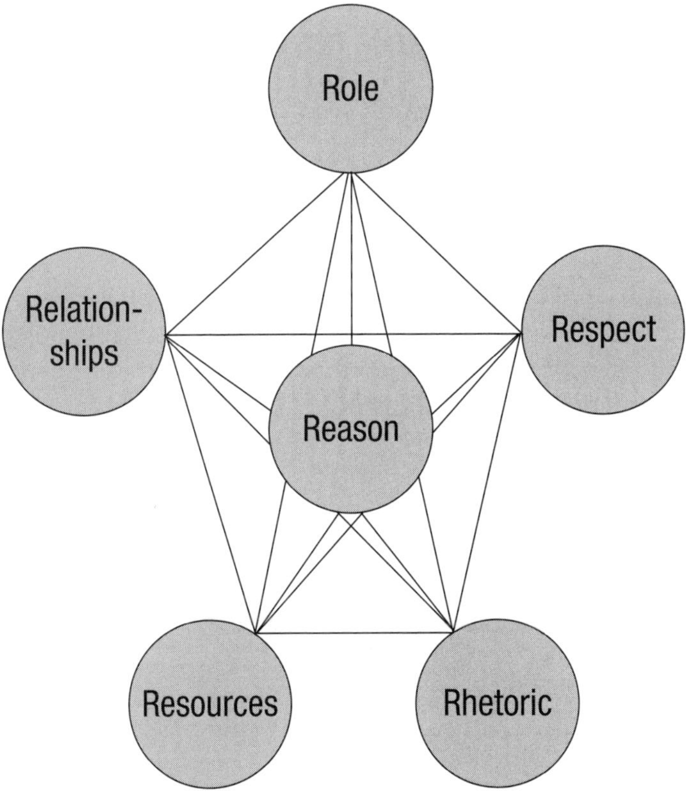

Adapted from *Enlightened Office Politics* by Michael and Deborah Singer Dobson (AMACOM, 2001).

· ·

HOW TO DO THESE EXERCISES

Most people have substantially more power than they know. However, they may not be conscious of the ways in which they drain their own power. The purpose of these questions is to get you thinking about your power assets and liabilities so that you become more conscious of how they work around you. You don't have to do them all. Some of them won't teach you anything you don't already know. Others may have limited bearing on your current situation and goals. Keep thinking about the questions you choose. You may need to come back to some of them again. Keep a notebook or journal (paper or electronic, as you prefer) in which you can jot down thoughts, ideas, and strategies as they occur to you.

· ·

EVALUATE YOUR REASON POWER

1. In what ways does your reason for seeking power increase your legitimate power?

_____

_____

2. In what ways does your reason for seeking power decrease it?

_____

_____

3. What are the potential benefits to others from your new power?

_____

_____

4. What are the potential negative effects on others from your power?

_____

_____

5. How could you improve your reason power?

_____

_____

6. Do you have enough reason power to achieve your goal?

_____

_____

ROLE POWER

Roles, both official and unofficial, are the source of what is known as "legitimate" power. This kind of power is delegated from others, not owned by you. If you leave the role, you don't get to take the power with you.

Some roles drain your power, of course, but they're found all over the hierarchy, not just at the bottom. In large organizations, there is usually a clerk who has immense power, and often a vice president without the power to order a box of staples. Entry jobs leading to great careers are highly desirable but at the same time powerless. Too many other people want that job.

Role power is relatively inflexible. It often isn't enough to get the job done. When you bolster role power with respect, rhetoric, and relationships, your power multiplies.

EVALUATE YOUR ROLE POWER

1. What roles do you play? Here are a few possibilities: job title, importance of the subject area (finance trumps warehousing), technical expert, committee member, project leader, educator/trainer, coach, and mentor.

_____

_____

2. For each role you write down, list its power effects—ways the role gives you power and ways the role saps your power.

_____

_____

3. If your role power is unsatisfactory, what roles should you seek instead? What do you have to do to get there?

_____

_____

4. What are the potential benefits to others from your role power, both current and desired?

_____

_____

5. What are the potential negative effects?

_____

_____

6. What effect does your role have on achieving your goal?

_____

_____

RESPECT POWER

Between the *Godfather* and Aretha, we've surely by now found out what r-e-s-p-e-c-t means to us.

Unlike role power, respect power is yours and yours alone. You can gain respect or others can lose respect for you. Also unlike role power, respect power is not constrained. There is no end to the respect you can earn (or lose), and there is no lack of category or opportunity.

You can win respect for your character, for your work, for your manners, for your knowledge, for your wisdom, for your friendliness, and so forth. We treat people with respect by listening to them, by consulting them where appropriate, by acknowledging their ideas and conclusions regardless of our final decision to use them, by using socially appropriate behavior, and more.

Not only do sources of power amplify or rob others, respect also influences respect. If we respect someone's technical expertise but not character or wisdom, the value we impart to the expertise is diminished.

Respect has rules. For example, as a rule of thumb, you can afford to show only about half the ego to which you're entitled before the ego cuts into the respect. There's little point in paying a compliment when the egotist has already sucked all the air out of the room. If someone doesn't show us the respect to which we're entitled, we tend to lower the respect we would otherwise proffer. Err on the side of treating people with more respect than you think they deserve.

Planning ways to increase respect is a highly productive activity. To earn real respect, you have to show real merit. You can't always depend on others to see the merit you display; they're busy demonstrating their own qualities. Don't err on the side of false modesty either. Other people may believe you.

EVALUATE YOUR RESPECT POWER

1. Write a list of categories in which you deserve respect. Some choices are character, skill, knowledge, wisdom, talent, decency, and courage. For each, why do you deserve respect? Be specific.

_____

_____

2. Do you have enough respect power to achieve your goal?

_____

_____

3. In what areas do people lack respect for you? Why? Are their perceptions correct in some ways? How could you change the situation or do you need a different situation?

_____

_____

4. How can you build on your strengths to gain the respect power you've earned? How can you moderate your weaknesses?

_____

_____

RHETORIC POWER

Communication skills are power. If you're a persuasive writer, if you're an effective negotiator—and if you're not intimidated by speaking in public—your power increases. Rhetoric—a slightly old-fashioned word that describes the discursive arts—is one of the original "3Rs."

As with respect power, you own the power your communication skills create. You can improve if you're willing to put in the work. Poor rhetoric drains power. If you've got great ideas and communicate them ineffectively, few of your ideas get picked up.

Communication is about far more than mere words. Research suggests that the words you speak account for only about 7 percent of what your audience takes in. The sound of your voice is far more powerful: 38 percent. If you tell people how happy you are and your voice sound morose, your listeners will assume you're being less than honest—even if you just talk that way. A whopping 55 percent of oral communication is visual. Body language, dress, grooming, and general appearance affect the listener's reaction and understanding in powerful ways.

Understanding human relations is another key to maximizing rhetorical power. What is the hidden agenda behind the innocent facade? What strategy will best influence my audience? Salespeople frequently role-play before a potentially difficult conversation; so should you.

One purpose of communication is to lower friction in relationships. If you're generally known as being friendly, assertive, and a good listener, you get a bonus to help you when the communication stakes are high. Paraphrase the other person and make sure he or she feels (and is) understood. He or she will be more likely to return the favor.

Know what you want to achieve. There are really only three reasons to communicate: you want someone to *know* something (convey or reinforce information, provide evidence); you want someone to *do* something (the nature of the action, reasons to take it, incentives, or persuasion); or you want someone to *feel* something (temporary or permanent feeling or opinion, degree of passion, reinforce current feelings, or change the direction of someone's sympathy or support).

Books and tapes abound. Organizations like Toastmasters are eager to help. You can attend seminars and workshops. And you can practice.

EVALUATE YOUR RHETORIC POWER

1. Assess your communication skills. What are your strengths, and can you build on them? What are your weaknesses, and can you compensate? Is there someone you can trust to give you an honest external perspective?

2. What role does rhetoric play in achieving your goal? Do you need to improve your skills? Will role-playing help?

_____

_____

3. What external factors get in the way of your communication (preconceived ideas, stereotypes, prejudices, organizational culture, conventional wisdom, beliefs, and opinions)? How can you adjust your approach to increase your chance of getting through?

_____

_____

4. How is your daily conversation? Do you make others feel heard? Do you make others feel valued? Are your efforts improving the willingness of others to listen to you and do as you suggest?

_____

_____

RESOURCE-DRIVEN POWER

If you control access to someone powerful, if you decide who gets which window office, or if you buy large quantities of goods for your organization, you get power. Like role power, resource-driven power usually involves control of someone *else's* goodies. The power is yours only temporarily.

The power advantage of controlling resources is obvious, but it's all too easy to fall into the trap of using the power to reward friends and punish enemies—especially the latter. The saying "Keep your friends close and your enemies closer" isn't just about keeping an eye on potential threats. (Why should they want to let you close if that's your only motive?) You keep your enemies closer to build improved relationships and negotiate mutual interests and goals. You keep your enemies closer so you can keep misunderstandings from hemorrhaging into unnecessary conflict. You keep your enemies closer because you don't really want enemies at all.

Be generous, at least as generous as your control and situation allow. Generosity fosters better relationships, lowers tension and negativity, and builds trust. Don't make quid pro quo a part of the transaction. Most people want to return favors if they can, and it's worth learning about the few who don't.

EVALUATE YOUR RESOURCE-DRIVEN POWER

1. What resources do you need to achieve your goal?

_____

_____

2. What resources do you control, either partially or totally? (Consider access, information, approvals, money, and tools and equipment.)

_____

_____

3. For each resource you control, who needs or wants some? What is the minimum you have to supply? What is the maximum? What value does the resource have for other people?

_____

_____

4. How can you get the resources you need for your goals?

_____

_____

RELATIONSHIP POWER

Whom you know matters. It matters a lot. Some people have an imperfect understanding of the power of relationships—they only *suck up*. Really powerful people know all sorts of people from CEOs to janitors, remember their names, and keep track of their personal details. People up, down, and sideways can all add to your power to get things done.

Make lists of people who may be able to help you in some part of achieving your goals. People can give you knowledge, an honest outside perspective, an introduction, advice, assistance, access, and much more. This does not mean treating people as if their only value is in what they can do for you. As noted earlier, open-handed generosity without expectation of reward is important. Cultivate people for their own sake; just don't be afraid to ask for help when there is something beneficial they can do for you. Many people view relational power as cynical and manipulative. It shouldn't be. You can't work with others without building relationships. You can build positive ones or negative ones. Obviously, the more positive ones you have, the better the work environment and the more gets done, including your goals. Focus on friendly relationship building first, and don't worry about the practical use of the relationship.

Think about this: Do you enjoy having the opportunity to help someone? Most of us do, and how much more pleasant it is to help people who've been friendly and thoughtful all along.

EVALUATE YOUR RELATIONSHIP POWER

1. List the people you know (this may take some time) and make sure they're in your address book. Add information such as names of spouses, children, pets; important dates; connections to one another; and your relationship with them. Memory is imperfect, and all of us have forgotten an important date at least once. Keep good records to supplement imperfect memory, and don't worry if you get caught at it. Let people know they're important enough to you for you to add memory aids.

_____

_____

2. Are there relationships you need to build or improve to achieve your goals?

_____

_____

3. Make a list of people you'd like to get to know, and add information about them in the same way. It's hard to open up a friendly conversation with a stranger, but if you can find a connection, conversation flows easily.

_____

_____

4. How can you use other sources of power (role, respect, resources) to connect to others and extend your network?

_____

_____

CHAPTER 12

PROJECT MANAGEMENT FOR GOAL ACHIEVERS

————————

The purpose of having a goal is to achieve it. To achieve it, you need a plan and the power to implement it. We've already discussed power and its relationship with achieving your goals. Now we need to know how to put power to use through careful planning. And planning falls under the heading of *project management*—managing temporary activities to achieve specific goals within the fundamental constraints of time, resources, and performance.

STEP 1—DEFINE THE GOAL

A goal, such as the goals you put together in the first section, usually needs to be fleshed out from a single sentence or short paragraph into a more detailed picture. We've learned that writing down our goal improves our likelihood of achieving it. Let's keep writing and come up with a deeper, fuller description of this project. Project managers call this the preliminary scope statement.

Consider some of these questions:

■ **Do we have an idea of what steps we'll have to take to achieve the goal?** For example, if I want to get a promotion, do

I need to take specific training or seek out a developmental job assignment?

■ **Are there constraints—things we *cannot* do even if they would be helpful in achieving the goal?** Obviously, I can't violate the law or ethical strictures. On the other hand, if there is a strict closing date in the next three weeks, I can't very well go get an MBA no matter how much it would help.

■ **Are we assuming things or taking things for granted when we think about this goal?** I may take for granted that Sue is not in the running for the promotion, but that is an assumption, not a fact. If I can find out, one way or the other, my plans may change. If I can't find out, I've got a risk. How should I manage that risk?

■ **Do we really understand *why* we want to achieve the goal?** Is this position my long-term goal or is it just a stepping-stone? If the latter, is it the only route I could take? Do I want the extra money? If so, how else could I earn more money? Is it the challenge? The power? Knowing why helps you see options, and it keeps you from pursuing a target that in the end won't give you what you truly want.

STEP 2—BREAK IT DOWN

Goals are usually too big to complete in a single step. You need to break the process into action steps, and then you need to string the steps together in order. The first part is called developing a *work breakdown structure* (WBS) and the second part is laying out a *network diagram.* (As we all know, it's important to have fancy technical names for basic tasks so they look sophisticated and mysterious!)

Let's develop a WBS (acronyms are even cooler) for a goal. The WBS lists and organizes the various tasks you need to do to achieve your goal. We'll use our example of getting a promotion. You pick any goal for which you've already developed a preliminary scope statement. You'll need sticky notes and someplace to stick them. (Flip chart paper is good, but you can also do it on a clean desk or worktable.)

Look over the example in Figure 12-1. You'll see it's pretty similar to an organization chart. Here's how to make your own.

Write the goal statement on a sticky note. That's the CEO level

FIGURE 12-1.   THE WORK BREAKDOWN STRUCTURE.

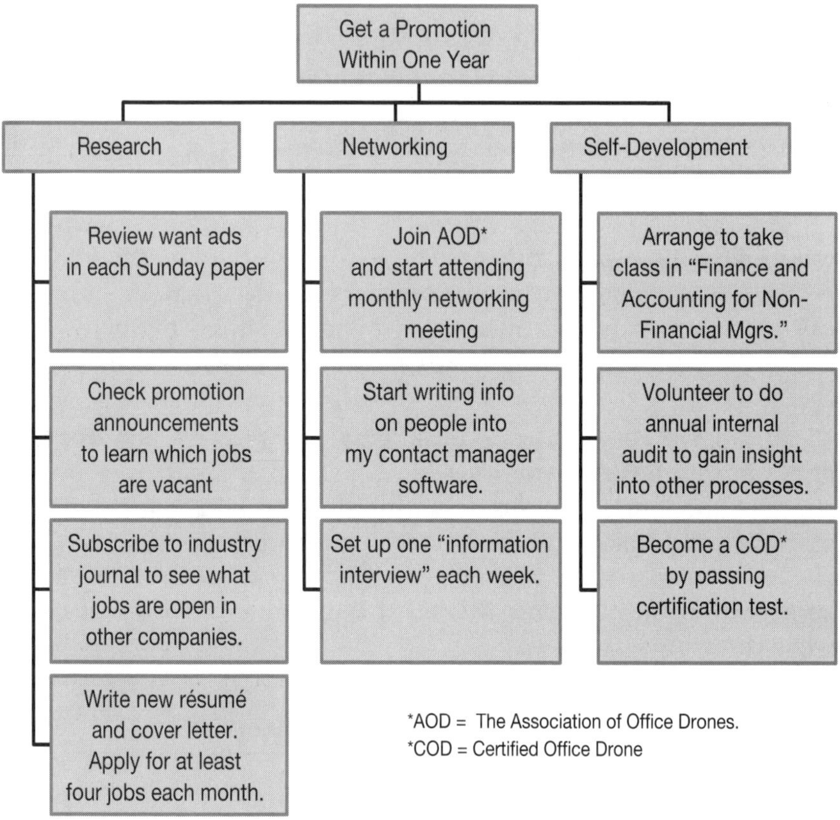

```
                    ┌─────────────────────┐
                    │   Get a Promotion   │
                    │   Within One Year   │
                    └─────────────────────┘
         ┌───────────────────┼───────────────────┐
┌──────────────┐   ┌──────────────┐   ┌──────────────────┐
│   Research   │   │  Networking  │   │ Self-Development │
└──────────────┘   └──────────────┘   └──────────────────┘
```

Research	Networking	Self-Development
Review want ads in each Sunday paper	Join AOD* and start attending monthly networking meeting	Arrange to take class in "Finance and Accounting for Non-Financial Mgrs."
Check promotion announcements to learn which jobs are vacant	Start writing info on people into my contact manager software.	Volunteer to do annual internal audit to gain insight into other processes.
Subscribe to industry journal to see what jobs are open in other companies.	Set up one "information interview" each week.	Become a COD* by passing certification test.
Write new résumé and cover letter. Apply for at least four jobs each month.		

*AOD = The Association of Office Drones.
*COD = Certified Office Drone

of your WBS. If you already know the best categories, write them each down on separate sticky notes. Those become the vice-president level. You'll then list the individual activities (staff) under each column. (By the way, you don't always have to limit yourself to three levels. Although it's not a good idea to have unnecessary levels, sometimes you need a little more detail.)

Now, sometimes you don't know yet how you should organize the tasks. If that is the case, do it backward. Write down all the tasks first, then figure out the best categories afterward and organize accordingly. What are the best categories? They're the categories that are useful to you when you do the work. For example, the items under *research* all need some private time for reading, and you probably need to write down the information you extract. You'll need to write cover letters and résumés.

. . . .

TIP!

You'll usually think of steps you missed as you go through the planning steps. For example, I (Michael) realized when I typed the sentence, "You'll need to write cover letters and résumés," that I hadn't actually listed that as part of the project. I quickly edited the figure to add the missing information.

This is not a problem, it's an opportunity.

A big part of going through the planning process is to focus your own thinking about your project. Each step almost always makes you think twice about what you did earlier, and it's not only okay to change, it's necessary. In fact, when the next planning step you take doesn't teach you or remind you of something new, that is a good benchmark to let you know when you've planned well enough.

. . . .

A WBS is done when it describes all the work necessary to accomplish the goal. Of course, making sure you've hit that point can be challenging, especially when the subject matter is unfamiliar to you. Consider waiting a few days before finalizing it. You may think of things you missed at any time. Keep something handy at all times to allow you to write down your thoughts, whether you prefer a low-tech pocket notebook or a high-tech PDA smartphone.

STEP 3—PREPARE A NETWORK DIAGRAM

A network diagram is sort of a flow chart of your project. It's the order in which you need to do the tasks. Figure 12-2 shows the research part of our promotion strategy presented in this form.

Tasks in your project can be *parallel*, which means they can take place at the same time as long as you have enough resources. Tasks are *dependent* if one or more other tasks have to be complete before the following task can be started. As you'll note in Figure 12-2, to apply for at least four jobs a month, we'll need to complete the three predecessor activities to find the necessary job leads.

Your network diagram has to make logical sense. Upon taking a closer look at Figure 12-2 you can see a logic problem. Although cover letters should be unique for every job, we probably need to prepare a more general-purpose résumé first. In other words, we

FIGURE 12-2.   NETWORK DIAGRAM FOR A PROMOTION.

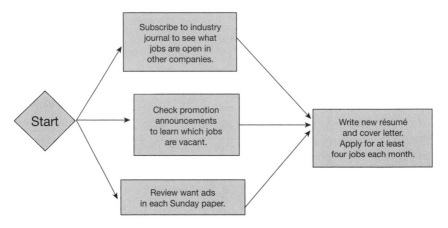

have to break the last task into different pieces and move one of them earlier in our network diagram, as shown in Figure 12-3.

The revised workflow makes more sense this way. Sticky notes are particularly valuable for this step, because you often need to revise your thinking as you work forward in the process.

FIGURE 12-3.   REVISED NETWORK DIAGRAM.

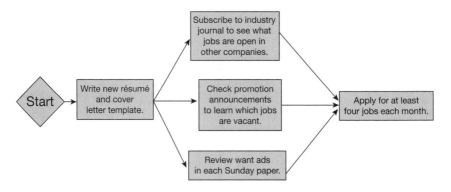

STEP 4—MAKE A SCHEDULE

If you don't get specific about when you plan to do these activities, you probably won't get around to doing them at all. You need a schedule.

There are two ways you can develop a schedule. The first is to enter the activities into your existing calendar. Making a date with yourself to do a task increases the odds of success. If you plan to wait until you get around to it, your chances are less. ("Round Tuits" are a frequent sight in country gift stores, which tells us how common the problem is. Sadly, there is no evidence that owning a round tuit actually aids goal accomplishment.)

Entering activities in your calendar makes sense when the tasks are short (no more than a couple of hours), repetitive (every week), and not full-time. If you need to spend significant full-time effort on each task, you'll find the Gantt chart a more useful way to keep things straight.

Our research and job application plan fits the first category. It's best to schedule these activities in a calendar format.

Remember, though, that one of our items is to volunteer to do the internal audit. It may be a difficult job, but you'll get noticed by decision makers and you also have the opportunity to learn all the nuts and bolts of your own operation. It's a valuable investment in your future.

For a period of time, this internal audit project is likely to be your life. You will probably want to break down the tasks within this area. Unlike "check the want ads every Sunday," the tasks in internal audit are pretty much full-time and they're work-related. Although you could certainly write "review documents" on every calendar page for two weeks, that isn't very helpful. Instead, you'll want to schedule interruptions in your calendar, and you'll want to develop a special form of schedule known as a Gantt chart. A Gantt chart is basically a bar graph drawn of a time line. It's better than a simple calendar when your activities are ongoing and take up a substantial amount of each day. Figure 12-4 shows an example for the internal audit.

STEP 5—ANALYZE YOUR RISKS

Although it would be nice to believe that your schedule will run smoothly and effortlessly, that's not the way to bet. Your project is subject to two kinds of risks: threats and opportunities. Threats cause damage to your project and may make it difficult for you to achieve your goals. Opportunities have potential benefits if you act on them. An example of a threat on the promotion project might be that a lot of other people may have an interest in the same job. An opportunity might come when you hear that someone is getting ready to leave, and it's a job you want.

FIGURE 12-4.   GANTT CHART.

	Jan 1	Jan 15	Feb 1	Feb 15

Volunteer to do internal audit ◇

Gather all necessary records ▬▬

Conduct a document review ▬▬▬▬

Conduct interviews ▬▬

Prepare report ▬▬

Develop recommendations ▬▬▬

Finish ◇

1. Identify Your Major Risks

What are the risks you're facing? Think about threats and opportunities, about what has happened on previous, similar projects, about who can give you good information about what you may be up against. Not sure if it's really a risk? Write it down anyway, and filter it out later. You don't need answers to your risks, at least not in this step.

2. Filter and Rank Your Risks

Generally, *threat risk* is bad. If you can avoid a threat risk (also known as pure risk) at a reasonable and proportional cost, it's a good idea to do so. *Opportunity risk*, on the other hand, is desirable. If you can take advantage of it—still at a reasonable and proportional cost—you're better off. *Business risk* combines threat and opportunity in the same choice. If you let your boss know someone's approached you about taking a job in another company, your boss might give you an immediate raise to keep you around—or may be happy to hold the door for you as you leave.

The term *reasonable and proportional cost* is important in planning for risk. The value of a risk is calculated by multiplying the probability of the event by the damage or benefit that could result, as shown in Figure 12-5.

FIGURE 12-5.   THE RISK FORMULA.

$$R = P \times I$$

If there is a 10 percent chance your decision could result in the loss of $1,000, the value of the risk is 0.1 × $1,000, or $100. That means if you can get rid of the risk for less than $1,000, it's a good idea. Because not all consequences of an event can be expressed in financial terms, it's possible you should spend more than $100 on this risk, but if so, you need to think about the decision to spend the additional money.

One problem with risk is that you may not know what the likelihood is of a given event occurring or exactly what it might cost if the risk actually occurs. You have to approximate, and that makes risk decisions more . . . well, risky. For example, if there is a moderate probability of a small financial impact, you want to spend little time and money on it. However, if there is a serious probability of a huge financial impact, you may need to spend big bucks to mitigate that risk. Making decisions on vague information pretty much guarantees you'll be wrong at least part of the time.

Should you make conservative decisions to lower your risk, or accept greater danger in the hope of a big payoff? That decision only you can make, because each situation is unique. To test whether you should go for it or be careful, answer the following four questions:

If I make this decision:

1. What's the best that can happen?

_____

_____

2. What's the worst that can happen?

_____

_____

3. Is number one worth risking number two?

_____

_____

4. Can I live with number two if it happens?

_____

_____

In question number three, the *worth* can be measured in many different ways. If the best outcome is significantly more probable or has a much greater relative impact, that should tilt our decision toward a yes answer. On the other hand, if the flow goes the other way, we might want to lean toward answering no.

If neither of these tests helps you decide, then look at the options. If I don't take this particular risk, what would I do instead? When Butch Cassidy and the Sundance Kid were on the top of that cliff in the Newman-Redford movie, thinking about jumping into the river far below, why were they considering such a risky strategy? Well, if they didn't jump, the posse would surely kill them. They had the likelihood of death on one hand, and the certainty of death on the other. That's not exactly a pleasant choice, but it's not a difficult one, either.

Don't confuse *worth* with an amount of money. If you could risk $5,000 of your money for a 70 percent chance of getting $50,000, traditional risk calculations would tell you to take the bet. Here's the formula:

$$EMV = (0.7 \times \$50,000) + (0.3 \times -\$5,000)$$
$$= \$35,000 + (-\$1,500)$$
$$= \$33,500$$

The expected monetary value of this investment takes into account the probabilities of winning or losing as well as the amount at stake. Here, the value of winning is the probability (0.7) times the amount ($50,000), which equals $35,000. The value of losing, on the other hand, is a 30 percent chance of losing $5,000, or $-\$1,500$. Add the numbers together to get $33,500. That's what you'd get on average if you could make the same investment over and over and over again. Notice that is a theoretical number. You actually get only a single bet. You'll get $50,000 or you'll lose $5,000.

Now, if you're an active investor with money in the bank, this is a pretty sweet deal. On the other hand, if it's your last $5,000 and you have rent to pay and food to buy, you can't afford to make the investment. The negative consequences of losing $5,000 are, in this case, greater than the benefits of winning $50,000. *Worth* and *amount* are not the same.

Numbers are extremely valuable contributors to good decision making, but don't let numbers make your decisions for you.

Develop Your Response Strategies

There are only a limited number of strategies you can use to manage your risks, whether threats or opportunities.

Strategies for All Risks (Threats and Opportunities)

1. **Acceptance**. Don't deal with the risk unless it actually happens. Best strategy when risk is unlikely and response expensive.

■ *Passive*. If the risk occurs, figure out an answer.

■ *Active*. Develop a contingency plan and trigger to use if necessary.

Strategies for Threat Risks

1. **Avoidance**. Change the plan so the risk either can't occur or won't have any impact. Best if avoidance is inexpensive or if impact is unacceptable.

2. **Transfer**. Give the risk to someone else. Insurance, for example, involves transfer of risk. The insurance company will take on your financial risk for some event (say, being in a car accident) in exchange for a premium, which is the actual value of the risk plus the costs of administration, marketing, and profit. Most risk transfer involves money, but "kicking the decision upstairs" transfers all kinds of risk, not merely money.

3. **Mitigation**. Mitigation strategies lower risk but don't eliminate it. If you're planning a picnic, one risk is that it might rain. If you rent a tent, the probability of rain is unaffected, but the impact is reduced. You don't get soaked, but the planned activities can't take place. On the other hand, if you schedule a rain date, you've lowered the probability of rain (but not eliminated it), but the impact stays the same. Mitigation is different from active risk acceptance, because you have to rent the tent in advance and pay for it whether or not it rains. If we're all going over to Christina's house if it rains on picnic day (contingency plan), she's safe from the hordes if there's not a cloud in the sky.

Strategies for Opportunity Risks

1. **Enhancing**. You may decide to grow a small opportunity into a big one by moving probability or impact higher. If there is a small chance of being considered for this great job, you might in-

crease your odds by applying through many different channels or you might increase the impact by checking industry salary standards so you know what you can ask for.

2. **Exploitation**. Cash in the opportunity in its current form. If one of your stocks suddenly skyrockets, you might sell it, especially if you're convinced it's at or near its top.

3. **Sharing**. If you're ahead on your project, you can offer to lend a hand to someone else, sharing the benefit of time saved. This is particularly powerful when the benefit is worth more to someone else than it is to you.

Implement the Plan

When you get the early warning signs that a risk event you've foreseen is about to happen, your risk plan has a ready response. If the risk plan turns out to be inadequate, you may need to take additional steps. If it's clear that certain risks can't happen any more, you may be able to shift resources. If new risks show up on the horizon, you can add them to the existing plan.

STEP 6—GET BUSY

You may need to edit your plan a bit based on your risk analysis, but once that's done, you're ready to go. You know what you're going to do, why you're going to do it, when each step needs to be accomplished, and where your dangers and problems are lurking.

Knowing how to plan is one of life's most valuable tools. Time spent planning is almost always a good investment. It saves going down wrong paths, walking into the jaws of obvious problems, and bumping around in the dark trying to find your way. Plans make you wiser about your own goals. Plans provide an incentive to other people to do their part for your goals.

Plans are imperfect and invaluable. The imperfections stem from our inability to read the future, so it's vital to stay flexible and alert. Even though we can't know everything about what is to come, we aren't helpless in the face of the unknown. We can prepare, we can organize, we can study our likely risks, and our plan will light the way to our eventual goal.

APPENDIX: GOAL ACHIEVEMENT WORKSHEET

The Goal. Describe the goal.

_____

_____

S-M-A-R-T Test: Make sure the goal fits each element of SMART.

Specific _____

Measurable _____

Agreed to _____

Realistic _____

Time-specific _____

Reason. Why do you want to achieve this particular goal?

_____

_____

Power. What kind of power do you need to achieve your goal? What power do you currently lack? Develop a plan to improve your power to get it done.

_____

_____

Assumptions. Things you believe about your situation, your plan, or your goal that you don't currently know for sure are true. (*Example.* My boss knows how hard I worked on the Glockenspiel deal. Are you sure? What makes you think so? Could the boss have noticed only some of your work?)

_____

_____

Constraints. Things you can't do. Make sure you really "can't do" them. Is there another way to get the same desired result?

_____

_____

List Action Steps/Develop Work Breakdown Structure. What do you have to do to accomplish the goal? If it's a complex goal involving several departments, a simple list of action steps may not be enough to capture what needs to be done. Use a WBS instead.

_____

_____

Develop Time Line and Budget. Use a calendar or Gantt chart to schedule the action steps. Identify the resources you have available and decide how best to use them.

_____

_____

Prepare Risk Plan. What are the key risks? How could you eliminate them in advance? How will you respond to them?

_____

_____

Verify Progress. Are you accomplishing what you set out to accomplish? What milestones or signposts show your progress most clearly?

_____

_____

Celebrate Success. Reward yourself and the people who helped you succeed. Even if it's an interim goal, celebrating your success today helps you move forward to another success tomorrow.

_____

_____

INDEX

Announcing!